The Assessment Papers

Spend some time talking with your child so that they understand the p
papers and how doing them will help them to prepare for the actual e:

Agree with your child a good time to take the assessment papers. This
and alert. You also need to find a good place to work, a place that is cc
distractions. Being able to see a clock is helpful as they learn how to pace themselves.

Explain how they may find some parts easy and others more challenging, but that they need to have
a go at every question. If they 'get stuck' on a question, they should just mark it with an asterisk and
carry on. At the end of the section, they may have time to go back and try again.

As in the actual test, the answers to the practice tests and assessment papers should not be written
on the question paper. They should be marked on the separate answer sheet (as in the real test a
computer will be used in the marking process). Answers should be carefully marked in pencil with a
straight line on the answer sheet.

Answer sheets for the practice tests and the assessment papers can be found at the very back of
the book on pages 153–160. Further copies of these answer sheets can be downloaded from
collins.co.uk/11plus.

How much time should be given?
The time allowed is given on the introductory pages at the beginning of each section. These timings
are based on the challenging time allocations that can be expected in an 11+ test. CEM tests are
designed to be time pressured and you don't necessarily need to complete all the questions to pass or
do well.

If your child has not finished after the allocated time, ask them to draw a line to indicate where they
are on the test at that time, and allow them to finish. This allows them to practise every question
type, as well as allowing you to get a score showing how many were correctly answered in the time
available. It will also help you and your child to think about ways to increase speed of working if this
is an area that your child finds difficult. If your child completes a section in less than the allocated
minutes, encourage them to go through and check their answers carefully.

Marking
Award one mark for each correct answer. Half marks are not allowed. No marks are deducted for
wrong answers.

If scores are low, look at the paper and identify which question types seem to be harder for your
child. Then spend some time going over them together. If your child is very accurate and gets correct
answers, but works too slowly, try getting them to do one of the tests with time targets going
through. If you are helpful and look for ways to help your child, they will grow in confidence and feel
well prepared when they take the actual exam.

Please note: As the content varies from year to year and county to county in CEM exams, a good score
in the assessment papers of this book does not guarantee a pass. Likewise, a lower score may not
necessarily suggest a fail.

**Collins is not associated with CEM in any way. This book does not contain any official questions and
it is not endorsed by CEM.**

**Our question types are based on those set by CEM, but we cannot guarantee that your child's actual
11+ exam will contain the same question types or format as this book.**

Acknowledgements

The authors and publisher are grateful to the copyright holders for permission to use quoted materials and images.

Page 51, Extract from *The Limpopo Academy of Private Detection* by Alexander McCall-Smith © 2013. Alexander McCall-Smith, published by Abacus Books.
Page 55, Extract from *Wicked* by Gregory Maguire. © 1995 Gregory Maguire. Reproduced by permission of Headline Publishing Group.
Pages 122–123, *Mount Yasur: To Hell and Back* © James Draven 2020

Every effort has been made to trace copyright holders and obtain their permission for the use of copyright material. The authors and publisher will gladly receive information enabling them to rectify any error or omission in subsequent editions. All facts are correct at time of going to press.

Published by Collins
An imprint of HarperCollins*Publishers*
1 London Bridge Street
London SE1 9GF

ISBN: 978-0-00-839888-0

First published 2020

10 9 8 7 6 5 4 3 2 1

British Library Cataloguing in Publication Data.

A CIP record of this book is available from the British Library.

Publishers: Clare Souza and Katie Sergeant
Contributing authors: Shelley Welsh, Faisal Nasim, Ian Kirby, Anne Rooney, Val Mitchell, Alison Head, Sally Moon and Richard F Toms
Project Development and Management: Richard S Toms and Rebecca Skinner
Cover Design: Kevin Robbins and Sarah Duxbury
Inside Concept Design: Ian Wrigley
Page Layout: Jouve India Private Limited
Production: Karen Nulty
Printed by: CPI Group (UK) Ltd, Croydon, CR0 4YY

MIX
Paper from responsible sources
FSC www.fsc.org FSC™ C007454

This book is produced from independently certified FSC™ paper to ensure responsible forest management.

For more information visit: **www.harpercollins.co.uk/green**

Contents

Introduction to Verbal Reasoning

You should be able to:

- solve problems that involve thinking about words and language
- understand the different meanings of words, including synonyms and antonyms
- understand a piece of writing
- identify the key pieces of information in the text: *who, what, when, where* and *why*.

What is Verbal Reasoning?

- Verbal reasoning involves solving problems based on words and language.
- Verbal reasoning questions will test your ability to understand and think things through logically.
- Verbal reasoning questions in the CEM test can be split into two main types: **comprehension** and **word choice**.

Comprehension

- 'Comprehension' means 'understanding'. A comprehension test gives you the chance to show you have understood a piece of writing and it is a key part of the CEM tests in verbal reasoning.
- Comprehension questions test your understanding of what a text says, its aims or purpose, its point of view and the way in which it gets information across.
- The questions may also test whether you understand when and where the events in the text take place – the context.

Comprehension: What to Expect

- Comprehension passages can be any type of writing but are most likely to be extracts from novels and poetry or non-fiction texts such as articles, recounts or instructions.
- You will need to work quickly – you may, for example, have 15 minutes to read a passage and answer 25 questions.
- All the questions are multiple choice: you just have to pick the right answer. Always make sure you read the question and all the answer options carefully before answering.
- Comprehension exercises test your understanding of what the text says **literally** – what it tells you directly – as well as what it **implies** or suggests.

Comprehension Skills

- In a comprehension test, you may need to work out:
  - **who** or **what** the text is about
  - **when** and **where** it takes place

> **Remember**
>
> Understanding starts with careful reading. Start by reading the text all the way through. Then, go through the questions one at a time, working out the answers by looking carefully at the text and finding the appropriate multiple-choice answer. If there are any questions you can't answer or aren't sure about, put an asterisk by them but make sure to select an answer option as you have a one-in-four chance of being correct. You can go back to them later if you have time.

- **why** the events happen or why the writer has written the information
- whose 'voice' the text presents.
- Skills for comprehension questions are covered on pages 8–35.

Word Choice: What to Expect

- CEM word choice questions are likely to be quite different to those that you have previously done at home or school.
- Most questions will be in multiple-choice format with at least four answer options to choose from.
- You will need to work quickly – for example, you may be asked to answer 25 questions in just 6 or 7 minutes.
- You cannot predict exactly which types of question will appear on the test but this book will help to build your skills for them.
- Word choice questions that you should be ready for include:
  - **Word definitions:** identifying the correct definition for a word that is used in a given sentence.
  - **Word associations:** identifying the word that is most closely related to another word.
  - **Synonyms:** identifying the word that is closest in meaning to another word.
  - **Antonyms:** identifying the word that is least similar in meaning to another word.
  - **Odd one out:** identifying the odd word out within a group of words, based on their meanings.
  - **Cloze:** choosing the correct word, or words, to complete the gaps in a sentence or passage.
  - **Shuffled sentences:** reordering a series of mixed-up words and finding which one of the words is not needed to form a correct sentence.

Word Choice Skills

- You will need to be able to think carefully and quickly about the precise meanings of words.
- Since many words in the English language have several alternative meanings, you will need to consider the context if they are used within a sentence.
- It is unlikely you will know the answer to all questions straight away, so you will need to consider the multiple-choice options and eliminate those that you know to be incorrect. Even if you are not sure of the meanings of all the words you are given, you can close in on the correct answer by discounting others.
- Strong spelling, grammar and punctuation skills will also help you and may be tested directly.
- Skills needed for word choice questions are covered in further detail on pages 36–48.

> **Remember**
>
> Having a wide range of vocabulary will help you to succeed in verbal reasoning. You cannot revise which words will appear on the test but you can improve your range of vocabulary by reading different types of books and texts, and doing practice exercises like those in this book.
>
> Use a dictionary to help you find word definitions and use a thesaurus to find new words that mean the same or similar to another. You could write down new words as you find them and then try using them.

> **Remember**
>
> In the actual test, you will not answer the questions on the question booklet itself. You will use a separate answer sheet similar to those found in this book on pages 153–160.

Skimming and Scanning Text

You should be able to:

- use skimming skills to look through a text quickly to get a general idea of what it is about
- use scanning skills to find specific information.

Skimming

- Skimming means reading through a text quickly to get an overall idea of what it is about. You don't read every word.
- If the text has a title, this may give you an idea of what it is about. Otherwise, the first sentence may help you.
- Don't forget to skim any subheadings in the text – these can help give you a general overview of what the text is about.
- Skim the extract below.

> ### Safety First
>
> Swimming on this beach is safe at some times of year. In early spring, dangerous high tides are signalled by a red flag on the beach. Do not swim if you see the flag. In late spring, the main dangers are sharks and jellyfish. Don't go in the water in April when these creatures most often visit. From May to August you should only swim when the lifeguard is on duty. There will be a green flag on the beach at these times. Never swim in a thunderstorm. In autumn, the sea may be rough. There will be a red flag when it is considered dangerous. If you see someone get into trouble in the water, call the lifeguard on this number: 999. There is a lifebelt under this notice.

Scanning

- Scanning means looking for particular words or phrases that might be relevant to the multiple-choice questions. You should look quickly at each sentence or paragraph to see if it is likely to contain the information you need to answer a question.
- As you get used to scanning, you'll find the words you're looking for 'jump' out of the text at you.

> **Example**
> What dangers and safety precautions are mentioned in the passage above? Highlight the key words and phrases.
>
> *In early spring, dangerous high tides are signalled by a red flag on the beach. ... In late spring, the main dangers are sharks and jellyfish... you should only swim when the lifeguard is on duty. There will be a green flag ... Never swim in a thunderstorm. In autumn, the sea may be rough.*

Remember

You probably skim and scan some texts already. If you look at the TV listings to pick a programme or film to watch, you don't read the descriptions of items that don't interest you – you scan for the names of programmes you like.

Example
What is this text about?

The title, 'Safety First', tells you it's going to be about safety. The first line tells you that the text is about when it is safe to swim: 'Swimming on this beach is safe at some times of the year.'

- In a non-fiction text, some key words or tricky technical words may appear with an explanation in a footnote or glossary.
- Highlight the words and phrases that you think are relevant to the question. Refer to subheadings as these may contain the word or phrase you are looking for.
- Think about how you could use scanning skills to find information in the example below.

Zombie Poodle Attack

Zombie Poodle Attack adds new types of zombie dog to ZombieZoo. You can customise the Zombie Poodles in your attack team, choosing their colour, special powers, fur style and diet. If you have ZombieZoo2, you can add Poodle Attack. If you have ZombieZoo, you will need to upgrade to ZombieZoo2 first.

The game needs a disk drive and 80MB of free hard disk space.

> **Remember**
>
> If you're trying to work out the mood or feeling of a piece of writing, scan for words relating to sounds, smells, sights and feelings.

Example

Which version of ZombieZoo do you need to have if you want to install Zombie Poodle Attack?
You need to have ZombieZoo2 in order to add Poodle Attack. Look for sentences relating to the sort of information you want to find – sentences with 'ZombieZoo' in them.

What else does your computer need to run Zombie Poodle Attack?
The information about the technical requirements is separate from the main part of the text. It states that you need a disk drive and 80MB of free hard disk space.

> **Remember**
>
> Sometimes the information you need may be in a specific place. For instance, the ingredients of a food product are listed in an information box on the packet.

> **Quick Test**
>
> Skim and scan this newspaper article to answer the questions.
> *Sisters Helen and Angela Macguire surprised police when they caught a criminal red-handed. The girls were playing netball in their driveway when they saw a smartly dressed man fiddling with their neighbour's car. Quick-witted Helen realised he wasn't the owner and she sneaked into her home to call the police. Officers swiftly arrived and arrested the man at the scene.*
>
> 1. Which of these would be the best title for this article?
>   A Exciting Games in the Garden
>   B Sisters at Play
>   C Car Thief Foiled by Games Girls
>   D The Netball Game
> 2. 'Quick-witted Helen realised he wasn't the owner...'
>   What is meant by 'quick-witted'?
>   A Careless   B Funny   C Frightened   D Alert

Finding Information

You should be able to:

- find information in a sentence or paragraph in factual and fiction texts
- use scanning skills to locate specific words or phrases related to the question.

Understanding How to Find Information in Non-fiction Texts

- Non-fiction texts often present information clearly, for example, by using subheadings and bullet points to structure the text.
- Usually, the information is easy to find and understand – the text clearly tells you what you need to know. But sometimes you may need to think a little and interpret the text.
- Sometimes, you will come across unfamiliar words – these may be explained in a glossary or footnote.

Remember

Use your scanning skills to find words or phrases that may lead you to the test question answer.

Skills in Searching Non-fiction Texts

- In descriptive texts or accounts, read carefully to find the information you need. Scan for words that may lead you to the answer to the test question.
- Use any subheadings to help you narrow down your search.
- Look at the following description of how to build an igloo, then read through the questions and explanations below.

A House of Ice

The ice is compacted – the snow has been pressed together with a lot of force so that it is solid. The Alaskan Eskimo cuts blocks from the ice to make the igloo. The serrated knife that they use makes it possible to saw through even the hardest blocks of ice. The Eskimo builder layers their blocks of ice and can cement them together with water. Although the house is made of ice, it can be warm inside. It shelters the family from the wind, and the warmth of their bodies soon heats up the space inside.

- What type of knife does the Eskimo builder use?
  *The question is about the knife, so scan the text to find the word 'knife'. The third sentence tells you about the Eskimo's knife: 'The **serrated** knife that they use...'. You may not know what 'serrated' means but it is clear that it is an adjective modifying the noun 'knife'.*

- Why is the ice very hard?
  You won't always find the words from the test questions used directly in the extract. The first sentence in the extract explains why the ice is hard: 'compacted' and 'solid' are the clues you need. The ice is made of snow that has been pressed (compacted) and become solid.
- Who will live in the house?
  Sometimes, a sentence that seems to be telling you something else gives you the information you need. The igloo 'shelters the family from the wind'. This tells you that a family will live in the igloo, although the sentence seems to be about why the igloo is warm – the information about the family is just dropped in while the text explains how the ice-house can be warm.

Understanding How to Find Information in Fiction Texts

- Finding information in stories and poems may take a bit of detective work.
- Stories, poems and plays include descriptions about characters, places, events, moods and feelings.
- Sometimes you have to work out the answers from descriptions or from dialogue (speech).

Skills in Searching Fiction Texts

- Look at the following story extract, then read through the questions and explanations below.

> ### Chopping wood
>
> Ivan wrapped his scarf tightly around his face against the freezing fog and picked up the axe. He was always scared to chop wood in the dead of winter. Every night, he heard the bears growling with hunger in the forest that surrounded their hut. Every night, they seemed to get closer and hungrier. He was sure they were hungry for boys. He was shivering with fright as much as cold when he lifted the latch and stepped outside. Dark gathered around the corners of the hut and between the trees. The wolves would be out soon.
>
> "There is some soup left from yesterday you can have when you come back," called his grandfather. "If you add more water, you can stretch it to two bowls and we can share it." Ivan's tummy rumbled at the thought of soup, even if it was thin. Perhaps he could find some crusts to drop into it, too.

- Who is this story about?
  Scan the text to find the names of, or references to, any characters. Only two are mentioned: Ivan, from whose viewpoint events are told, and his grandfather.

> **Remember**
>
> In an instructional text, what you need and what you should do will be presented clearly. There may be footnotes, lists and numbered points to help you; for example, in a recipe, the ingredients are clearly listed at the start, and what you need to do is set out in steps.

- What is happening?

  What is happening is most likely linked to the main character, Ivan. Scan the text to find his name and see what he is doing: Ivan is getting ready to go outside and chop wood. He is looking forward to soup when he gets back.

- Which two of the following are reasons why Ivan is shivering?

  1 He is hungry   2 He has a fever   3 He is cold

  4 He is scared   5 He is exhausted

  A 1 and 2   B 1 and 3   C 2 and 3   D 3 and 4

  D: He is cold and he is also scared of the bears growling with hunger and the wolves that might be outside: he is 'shivering with fright as much as cold'.

- Why is Ivan particularly worried about the bears?

  Scan the text to find the word 'bears'. Ivan is worried that the bears may have a particular interest in eating boys: 'Every night, they seemed to get closer and hungrier. He was sure they were hungry for boys.'

- Where do you think Ivan and his grandfather live?

  Sometimes you can use information about what is happening in the story to help you answer questions. We are told that Ivan and his grandfather live in a hut in the forest, in an area where there are bears and wolves. You may know that Ivan is a Russian name and that Russia has a lot of forest, and there are bears and wolves there, so they may live in Russia.

Remember

Although your own experiences can help you to infer what the writer is saying, remember that the clues to the answer will be in the text. For example, we are not explicitly told that Ivan is hungry, but you can tell that he is hungry because his 'tummy rumbled at the thought of soup'.

Quick Test

Read this passage and answer questions 1–3.

Boat Crew in Trouble

An attempt to copy a historic journey made more than a thousand years ago was abandoned last night. A team of students from Southampton built a boat similar to one Polynesian explorers may once have used. The seven-person crew gave up 200 miles short of their destination and radioed for help.

"We had run out of drinking water," one crew member told our interviewer, "so we had to give up our goal of making it to Hawaii. It's a shame, but we will try again when we can raise the money for another attempt."

1. How many people were in the boat?

   A two   B three   C seven   D 200

2. Where was the boat supposed to be going?

   A Polynesia   B Hawaii   C Southampton   D France

3. When did Polynesian explorers go to Hawaii?

   A In 1974   B Last month   C In 1720   D More than 1000 years ago

Read this passage and answer questions 4 and 5.

The baby gurgled and waved its podgy arms around. It sat like a fat triangle on the rug, its nappy forming a solid base. Then it squealed loudly and made a lunge for the plastic bricks that Dom was playing with. Dom immediately held them out of the baby's reach. The baby squealed again, but this time it sounded different – it sounded cross. Dom smiled at it, a nasty, leering smile. The baby wasn't fooled and stretched out its hand to try to reach the plastic bricks, but Dom held them high in the air. The baby fidgeted on its bottom, but couldn't move closer. Dom moved further away, trying to tempt the baby into toppling over. At that moment, Rita came in, and Dom quickly hid the bricks behind his back.

"Are you two having a nice time?" she asked.

"Lovely," Dom lied. As soon as Rita turned her back, Dom poked his tongue out at the baby. The baby waved its arms again, still wanting the bricks, and began to cry. Dom smiled, and held the bricks even more tightly, but just where the baby could see them.

4. What is the baby wearing?

    A a sleepsuit **B** a dress **C** a nappy **D** a t-shirt

5. Which statement about Dom's feelings towards the baby is true?

    A He likes the baby – he passes the plastic bricks to it.
    B He likes the baby – he gives it a kind, friendly smile.
    C He dislikes the baby – he holds toys where the baby can't get them.
    D He dislikes the baby – he calls it fat and podgy.

Organisation of Text

You should be able to:
- understand how a text is organised.

Understanding How Text is Organised

- The organisation of a text refers to the way it is arranged in sentences and paragraphs, and how these are linked.
- Most texts follow a clear sequence with a beginning, a middle and an end. However, some texts – such as poems – have a more complicated or surprising organisation.
- Some texts, such as stories, may tell events out of sequence, using 'flashbacks' to take the narrative back in time from the current point.
- The title and any subheadings often help you see what a text is going to be about and how it is organised.
- Changes in font style, such as bold or italics, are often used to make text stand out or to emphasise a point.

Skills in Identifying How a Text is Organised

- Look at the following extract, then read through the questions and explanations that follow.

Fruity Flapjacks Recipe

What you need:
- o   800 g oats
- o   200 g brown sugar
- o   2 tablespoons syrup
- o   100 g butter
- o   100 g raisins or sultanas
- o   Handful of sesame and pumpkin seeds

Top Tip! If you have a sweet tooth, why not add some chopped glacé cherries?

Method:
1. First, place the oats, fruit and seeds into a large mixing bowl.
2. Second, melt the sugar, syrup and butter in a pan.
3. Next, add the mixture to the oats, fruit and seeds and stir well.
4. Finally, turn the mixture into a greased baking tray and bake for 40 mins on gas mark 6, electric 180 degrees.

- How is the text organised to make it easier to read?
  The subheadings 'What you need' and 'Method' are written in italics and bold to make them stand out. The ingredients are listed in bullet points so you can see immediately what you need. Quantities are written at the start of each item, which means you can see clearly how much of everything you need. The method steps are numbered and start with time connectives so the order is clear.

- Why do you think the 'Top tip!' is written in a separate box?
  Your eye is drawn to it because it stands out from the rest of the text. It might have been too cluttered if it had been included in the list of ingredients or the method steps. Also, it is written in a more relaxed, informal style, addressing the reader with a question, so it makes sense for it to be separate from the rest of the text.

> **Remember**
>
> Words used to connect sentences and phrases organise the text into a sequence. Look for time connectives that tell you the order of events, such as 'before', 'after', 'when' and 'then'.

Quick Test

Read this passage and then answer the questions.

It's Raining Birds!

Residents of a small town in Arkansas were astonished to find dead birds falling from the sky. Over one evening and night, 3000 dead birds rained down on the town. On New Year's Day, local people woke to find dead blackbirds scattered all over the town. Experts called in to examine them were baffled.

Possible Reasons
Suggestions as to what killed the birds include:

- *pesticides*
- *fireworks*
- *thunderstorms*
- *hail*
- *flying into buildings.*

However, none of these explain the large number of deaths.

"It remains a mystery," said a spokesman. "We don't know what caused the rain of birds, or why they are concentrated in such a small area."

More Mystery
Bizarrely, reports of mass deaths of fish, birds, crabs and other animals have flooded in from around the world since New Year. Scientists have not been able to come up with an explanation.

1. Which two organisational features are used in the passage?
   1 subheadings   **2** bullet points   **3** a spokesman   **4** adverbs   **5** conjunctions
   A 1 and 2   **B** 1 and 3   **C** 3 and 4   **D** 4 and 5

2. What does the article encourage you to think about the 'rain of birds'?
   A That the birds were killed by pesticides.
   B That the birds flew into buildings.
   C That scientists know how the birds died.
   D That the 'rain of birds' is a mystery.

Understanding Context

You should be able to:
- identify the context in which a text is written.

Understanding Context

- Texts often reflect the societies and cultures in which they are written or set.
- Context refers to the time and place in which a text was written or set; understanding the context will help you understand the text. For example, people often travelled in vehicles pulled by horses in the 19th century, so this mode of transport would probably indicate that a story is set a long time ago.
- Some texts have a traditional form of opening; for example, many fairy tales start with 'Once upon a time…'.
- A fable tells a short story and then explains the moral that is being addressed. Look out for traditional contexts like these – they tell you the type of story you are reading.

Skills in Understanding Context

- Look at the following extract, then read through the questions and explanations below.

A Prison Ship

The boat had returned, and his guard were ready, so we followed him to the landing place made of rough stakes and stones, and saw him put into the boat, which was rowed by a crew of convicts like himself. No one seemed surprised to see him, or interested in seeing him, or glad to see him, or sorry to see him, or spoke a word, except that somebody in the boat growled as if to dogs, "Give way, you!" which was the signal for the dip of the oars. By the light of the torches, we saw the black Hulk lying out a little way from the mud of the shore, like a wicked Noah's ark. Cribbed and barred and moored by massive rusty chains, the prison ship seemed in my young eyes to be ironed like the prisoners. We saw the boat go alongside, and we saw him taken up the side and disappear. Then, the ends of the torches were flung hissing into the water, and went out, as if it were all over with him.

Great Expectations, by Charles Dickens

- What in this text tells you it is not about modern Britain?
  Look for clues that tell you the time and place in which the text was written or set. The title of the text may sometimes help. The things and people in the text and the way people talk to each other can give you clues about

the social and historical context. In this extract, the man goes in a boat rowed by prisoners to a prison ship. This doesn't happen today in Britain. Also, the men use flaming torches – today we use electric lights or battery-powered torches.

- What is the attitude towards the prisoners? Is this a modern British attitude?
  Look at the attitudes and viewpoint shown in the text. This may reflect the time and place it was written or set. The prisoners are treated badly – they have to row the boat, they live in a prison ship and they wear iron chains: 'the prison ship seemed in my young eyes to be ironed like the prisoners'. Someone growls at them as though they were dogs. Attitudes and behaviour towards prisoners in Britain today are quite different – prisoners have rights.

- What assumption does the writer make when choosing the phrase 'a wicked Noah's ark'?
  A writer might make assumptions about what the reader knows. These assumptions are based in the social and historical context of the writing. The writer here assumed his readers would know the Bible story of Noah's ark, so he was writing in a time and place when most people were Christians or at least familiar with Christianity.

Quick Test

Read this passage and then answer the questions.

Once upon a time, there was a beautiful girl who lived with her old father in a village in the forest. They were poor, but happy.

One day, the father had to go to the nearby town on business. He asked his daughter if there was anything she wanted as a present. Knowing they were poor, the girl asked for only a single rose, which she thought he would be able to pick from a rose tree.

On his way back, the father saw blood-red roses on a rose bush that leaned over a high wall. Thinking to take just one for his daughter, he followed the wall to a locked iron gate. Behind the gate was a huge, dark tower.

1. Which words in the first paragraph suggest that this text is the opening of a fairy tale?
   A Once upon a time
   B there was a beautiful girl
   C who lived with her old father
   D They were poor, but happy

2. Why do you think the girl asked only for a rose from her father?
   A She liked the smell of roses.
   B She thought it would look beautiful in the house.
   C The family did not have much money.
   D It would be easy to carry home.

Types of Comprehension Question

You should be able to:

- answer different types of multiple-choice comprehension questions.

Question Types

- The CEM reading comprehension papers contain a number of different types of multiple-choice question.
- These questions can focus on:
  - information retrieval
  - understanding meaning
  - inference and deduction
  - language definition
  - author's intentions and use of language
  - parts of speech.

Information Retrieval Questions

- These questions are straightforward recall questions where the answer can be found in – or retrieved from – the text. They might be short questions, starting with words like 'Who', 'What' and 'Which'.
- You will need to use your skimming and scanning skills to find the information you have been asked for, then select the correct answer option.

Understanding Meaning Questions

- These questions test your understanding of what the text says.
- You might be asked to choose the option that best summarises or paraphrases what has happened in the text, or why something has happened, to test your understanding.
- You could be given a quote from the text and asked to choose the option that explains what is meant.
- These questions may also test your wider knowledge and therefore it is important to read a wide range of text types as part of your practice for the tests.

Remember

Skimming means reading through a text quickly to get an overall idea of what it is about.

Scanning means looking for particular words or phrases. These might be words and phrases you need to answer a multiple-choice question.

Inference and Deduction Questions

- You will need to read between the lines to answer these types of questions, drawing on your own personal experience, knowledge or opinion.
- You could be asked to answer a question starting, 'Why do you think that…?' where the answer isn't obvious from the text; you will need to use your inference and deduction skills to be able to select the correct option.

Language Definition Questions

- These are questions about the meanings of different words as they are used in the text.
- You may be asked to pick the option that best defines the meaning of a word or phrase, or perhaps to choose a synonym or an antonym of a word.

Author's Intentions and Use of Language Questions

- These questions ask why the writer might have used specific words and phrases, e.g. the effect they wanted to create by describing the characters, setting or atmosphere in a particular way.
- It might be that the writer has used the weather as a backdrop to a story and you are asked to select an option about the effect that has been created, e.g. a storm when events are sinister creates a dark mood and sunshine during happy events creates a cheerful mood.

Parts of Speech Questions

- You will have covered a wide range of word classes as part of your grammar learning. These include: verbs, adverbs, nouns, adjectives, prepositions, pronouns and conjunctions.
- You might be asked a question where you will need to identify and select an answer that is one of these parts of speech – or word classes – so it is important that you know them.

Information Retrieval Questions

You should be able to:

- find specific information in the text to answer the question
- find information relating to character, setting and mood
- use scanning skills to find the part of the text you need.

Finding Information

- This type of question is straightforward because you are simply selecting information from the text that answers the question – the answer is in the text. They often begin with 'Who', 'What', 'Where,' 'When' or 'Why' (the five Ws).
- Information retrieval questions will be asked about both fiction and non-fiction texts. For both genres, you will need to use your scanning skills to find the information you need to answer the multiple-choice question. Some answers will be obvious while others might be trickier as the correct answer will be similar to other options in the multiple-choice list.
- When searching for specific words or phrases, you should scan the text and underline or highlight these words and phrases and those close in meaning. For example, if you were looking for answers about areas of water in a non-fiction text about global geography, you would underline or highlight the names of seas and oceans, as well as any other words linked to water such as 'river' or 'lake'.

Skills in Information Retrieval

- **Finding information about characters** – First, scan the text for proper nouns to find the name of the character or characters you are being asked about. Then look for specific information linked to the question.
- **Finding information about setting** – These questions can be more difficult as descriptions of setting are often woven into the text. Scan for words and phrases relating to the place or time in which the text is set.
- **Finding information about the mood** – Look for phrases, adjectives and adverbs that describe the action, characters, setting and events. These can quickly identify the mood.
- Look at the extract below then read through the questions and explanations that follow.

> We were all exhausted by the time we got to bed that night. The journey from Birmingham had been long and tedious, with lengthy delays on the M6. It's always like that on Christmas Eve. It was already dark when we arrived at my mother's cottage and the children – Joey, Amelia and Tom – were in bed by eight o'clock. I stayed up for another hour, talking to Mum and putting

the presents under the tree. I must have fallen asleep as soon as we got to bed.

The first indication that anything was wrong was when I heard a little voice saying, "Dad, Dad," over and over again, and woke to find Tom pulling at my arm. It was almost midnight. He said that he had heard a strange noise and was frightened. I listened. I could hear the whoosh of rushing water coming from downstairs. I opened the bedroom door and saw that the water was already halfway up the stairs.

- **Who** alerts the writer to the danger?
  The person who alerts the writer to the danger is Tom. Scan the text for references to a person's name or a personal pronoun to find someone who is interacting with the writer. Here, the narrator refers to waking up to find Tom pulling at his arm.
- **What** is the cause of the noise?
  The cause of the noise is the water. Scan the text for any reference to a noise. Here, it is 'the whoosh of rushing water'.
- **Where** is the family staying when the flood happens?
  The family is staying at the narrator's mother's cottage. Scan the text for a reference to a location. It is clearly not Birmingham as they are driving away from there. The next reference to a setting is '...we arrived at my mother's cottage'.
- **When** does the flood take place?
  The flood takes place on Christmas Eve, just before midnight. Scan the text for a reference to time. The narrator says they left Birmingham on Christmas Eve and when Tom woke the narrator 'It was almost midnight.'

Remember

Some answer options may *paraphrase* what is in the text. This means putting the words in the text into different words rather than copying exactly what is written.

Remember

Use your scanning skills to find words or phrases that may lead you to the answer.

Quick Test

Refer back to the passage above and answer these questions.

1. Why was the narrator exhausted when he went to bed that night?
   - A He had had to bail out the flood water.
   - B He hadn't had any sleep for days.
   - C He spent the evening searching for his mother.
   - D It had been a tiresome trip with motorway delays.

2. How is the narrator first alerted to the fact that something is wrong?
   - A Joey and Amelia tell him they have heard a whooshing noise.
   - B He hears the water flooding the cottage.
   - C His mother says she has heard a strange noise.
   - D He is woken up by his frightened son.

Understanding Meaning Questions

You should be able to:

- summarise what the text is about to show understanding
- choose the option that explains what is meant in a given quote from the text.

Understanding the Meaning of Texts

- These types of questions test your understanding of the text.
- You will often be asked to pick the option that best summarises what has happened or what the text is about.
- You may also be asked about the meaning of a quote or short extract from the text.

Skills in Summarising a Non-fiction Text

- After you have read through the text, use your skimming skills to go through it again if you aren't sure what it is about.
- Look at the following passage, then read through the questions and explanations below.

> Although archery is now principally a popular sporting activity, many people still use bows and arrows to participate in 'bow hunting'. Hunting prey, such as small and large game, involves the skills of stalking and understanding the habits of prey. Some fishermen also engage in spear fishing, which requires keen vision and the ability to calculate the position of the fish, accounting for how water distorts the visual image.

Remember

Some non-fiction texts might use a lot of technical language. Refer to the footnotes, if provided, and annotate the text if need be. Use the title and subheadings to help you work out what the text is about.

- Is the first part of the passage about the sport of archery or 'archery' as a type of hunting?
  It is about the use of bows and arrows to hunt prey.
- Why do the fishermen need to know how water distorts an image?
  So that they can calculate the exact position of the fish.

Skills in Summarising a Fiction Text

- After you have read through the text, think about the general meaning of the text, poem or extract.
- To help you, highlight or underline key words and phrases.
- Think about who or what the subject of the text is. Then consider what they are *doing*.

Remember

Use your scanning skills to find words or phrases that may lead you to the answer.

Quick Test

Read this passage and then answer question 1.

'Kidstech' – Laptops for All
Laptops for School Learning
As computers are now seen as an essential tool for learning, a campaign called Kidstech, established by parents, is putting pressure on the Government to provide each school child with their own laptop.

Exercise Over Laptops
Although this is a popular crusade, there is opposition: some doctors believe that exercise and outdoor games are more important for a child's development, citing evidence that indicates that computers are contributing to childhood obesity. They point out that the cost of providing computers would cut into school budgets and reduce funding for sports.

Laptops Aid Employment
On the other hand, statistics show that school leavers with restricted access to computers are 30 per cent less likely to find skilled employment.

1. Which summary best explains what the text is about?
   A   Schools encouraging parents to buy 'Kidstech' laptops to support their children's learning.
   B   A parental campaign called 'Kidstech' which wants schools to provide laptops for all children.
   C   The danger of children using the internet unsupervised.
   D   The expense of laptops and its impact on school budgets.

Read the poem and then answer questions 2 and 3.

'I Wander'd Lonely as a Cloud' by William Wordsworth

I wander'd lonely as a cloud
That floats on high o'er vales and hills,
When all at once I saw a crowd,
A host, of golden daffodils;
Beside the lake, beneath the trees,
Fluttering and dancing in the breeze.

Continuous as the stars that shine
And twinkle on the Milky Way,
They stretch'd in never-ending line
Along the margin of a bay:
Ten thousand saw I at a glance,
Tossing their heads in sprightly dance.

2. Which summary best explains what the poem is about?
   A   It is about someone who is flying in the air.
   B   It is about an astronaut in the Milky Way.
   C   It is about the thousands of stars in the Milky Way.
   D   It is about someone who comes across lots of daffodils.

3. What is meant by these lines?
   'Continuous as the stars that shine
   And twinkle on the Milky Way'
   A   The daffodils were as numerous and bright as the stars.
   B   The daffodils looked up towards the stars.
   C   The poet continued to look at the stars.
   D   The stars were like daffodils.

Inference and Deduction Questions

You should be able to:

- read between the lines to answer questions about a text
- use your own experience and knowledge to reach a conclusion
- look for clues about the story, characters and setting in a fiction text
- predict possible or likely outcomes from what the characters in a fiction text do, say and feel
- identify how the characters are feeling, and the mood and atmosphere created.

Understanding Inference and Deduction in Texts

- To infer (inference) means to use clues in the text, as well as your own personal knowledge, experience or opinion, to reach a conclusion about something that is not directly stated. Sometimes this is referred to as 'reading between the lines'.
- To deduce (deduction) is about being able to reach a conclusion based on factual information or evidence given in the text.
- Both test your ability to do more than just find information in a text.

Skills in Inference and Deduction

- To answer inference and deduction questions, you will need to collect all the supporting information and clues from the text that are linked to the question. These might be found in vocabulary; descriptions of characters, events, setting and moods; characters' actions and their dialogue.
- Questions that test your inference skills may start with phrases like, 'Why do you think the narrator supports the view that…?', 'What does the narrator suggest by…?', 'What is implied by…?'
- Questions that test your deduction skills may start with phrases like, 'How can you tell that…?', 'What clues tell you that…?'

Example

What can be **deduced** and **inferred** from this sentence?

On arrival at the scene, Police Constable Javid found a cyclist lying motionless at the side of the road, a mangled bike and a concerned motorist.

*You can **deduce** that there has been a serious accident because there is a cyclist who is not moving, a damaged bike and a police officer has arrived.*

*You can **infer** that the motorist has been involved in a collision with the cyclist, though there isn't enough evidence to be certain – it is possible that the motorist was simply passing by and stopped when he or she saw the injured cyclist at the roadside.*

Remember

Inference is what you think has happened and deduction is what you can be sure has happened given the clues.

- Look at the following **non-fiction** passage, then read through the questions and explanations below.

Bears

Bears are mammals that are found throughout North America, South America, Europe and Asia. Some are as tall as 2.5 m and can weigh up to 500 kg. Bears have large, strong jaws, an excellent sense of smell and long paws with non-retractable claws. They are solitary animals, except for mothers with their cubs. Bears can live up to 25 years in the wild and 50 years in captivity.

- The text tells us that bears can be as tall as 2.5 m and weigh up to 500 kg. What else tells us that bears could be dangerous animals?
Find other facts about bears and ask yourself if these imply that bears are dangerous. Remember, not all the facts will imply or suggest this. The words 'large, strong jaws ... and long paws with non-retractable claws' suggest, without stating it explicitly, that the bear is a potentially dangerous animal. However, their 'excellent sense of smell' and the fact that they are 'solitary animals' don't imply danger.

- Look at the following **fiction** passage, then read the questions and explanations below.

> Mrs Whitham's maid opened the door and ushered her into the hallway. She took her wet umbrella from her and led her gently into the parlour. "My word, ma'am, what a day!" exclaimed Sally, settling Mrs Whitham comfortably into her chair by the fire. Mrs Whitham's wrinkled face lit up into a smile as she warmed her cold, paper-thin hands in front of the flames while Sally unpicked the slide from her grey hair.

- How do we know that Mrs Whitham is elderly?
Search for descriptions that suggest the character's age. Scan the text for adjectives, adverbs and phrases. The fact that Mrs Whitham has a 'wrinkled face', 'paper-thin hands' and 'grey hair' are clues and evidence that she is elderly.
- What was the weather like?
There may not be a sentence or phrase that actually tells you, but there may be something that hints at the weather. Scan the text for evidence – the fact that Mrs Whitham's umbrella was wet is a clue that it was raining. And Mrs Whitham warming her cold hands in front of the flames is evidence that it was cold outside.

> **Remember**
>
> When you **imply**, you hint or suggest something; when you **infer**, you use the information supplied to make an educated guess. The writer **implies** and the reader **infers**.

> **Remember**
>
> Do not just pick an answer because it provides a true statement about something that you have some knowledge about – it must answer the question.

Predicting Outcomes

- To predict outcomes in a text, you will need to use your own prior knowledge or find clues that hint at something that may be about to happen.
- Read this sentence:

  Frida eyed up the height of the wall, looking behind her to make sure Mum wasn't watching.

  What do you think will happen next? Think about what might be going through Frida's mind: why would she want to make sure Mum wasn't watching?

Identifying Feelings and Moods

- It is important to be aware that what characters say is not always what they feel. Look at this short passage, then read through the explanation:

  "I thought you said you had a date," said Dad to Idra as she began stacking the dishwasher.

  "It's fine, Dad," sighed Idra, shooting an anxious glance at Mum.

  - How did Idra really feel?

    Look for language that reveals emotions. The word *'sighed' might imply that Idra was sorry she was missing her date but felt she should help Mum, even though she says 'It's fine'. 'Shooting an anxious glance at Mum' implies that she may be worried about her mother (she may be unwell).*

- Writers sometimes tell you about the mood in a text by describing other things such as the weather or the setting. Look at this short passage, then read through the explanation:

  As Ronan and Sian ran frantically from the dark depths of the woods, the lightning continued its stabbing punishment and the thunder rolled angrily.

  - What mood is conveyed by the writer?

    Look for language that is used to describe how the characters behave and the setting and/or weather. The adverb 'frantically' implies a sense of panic; 'dark depths' makes the woods seem scary and foreboding; the personification of the lightning with its 'stabbing punishment' and the thunder, which 'rolled angrily', makes the weather seem actively aggressive. The mood that is created helps to convey to the reader the danger that Ronan and Sian are in.

> **Remember**
>
> Sometimes additional information about a person's character will be implied by clues in the text, such as:
>
> - what the character does / how the character behaves
> - how others react to them
> - what characters say / how they speak.

Quick Test

Read the extract and then answer the questions.

The station clock said 3pm. Emerging from the sea of bustling travellers, Gwendoline slowly unlinked her hand from her mother's and walked with some hesitation towards the train. She bit her bottom lip and stepped into the carriage. It didn't take long for her to find her allocated seat, fortunately on the platform side. After she had placed her case on the luggage rack, she peered out of the window, fixing her eyes on her mother who was dabbing her moist cheeks with a handkerchief. The guard's whistle blew; the train trudged off. Gwendoline sobbed and fixed her eyes on her mother until she became a distant pinprick. Pressing her hot cheek against the cool window, she put her hand in her coat pocket and fiddled with the silver charm her mother had given her before they had left home. Would it bring her good fortune?

1. Why is it *fortunate* that Gwendoline's seat is on the platform side?
   A She could see the station clock.
   B She was able to wave goodbye to her mother.
   C She just preferred the platform side.
   D She could wave to the guard.

2. What tells you that Gwendoline's mother was sad to wave her daughter goodbye?
   A She bit her bottom lip.
   B She gave her a silver charm.
   C She had moist cheeks.
   D She became a distant pinprick.

3. Why do you think Gwendoline's cheek might be hot?
   A She has a temperature.
   B It's hot in the carriage.
   C It's a summer's day.
   D She has been crying.

Language Definition Questions

You should be able to:

- identify the meaning of words and phrases as they are used in a text
- know what synonyms are and be able to identify them in a text
- know what antonyms are and be able to identify them in a text.

Identifying the Meanings of Words and Phrases

- Your CEM test could include questions about the meanings of different words and phrases as they are used in the text, including picking the option that best defines their meaning.
- You may also be asked to select a synonym or an antonym for a particular word.
- When you are asked about the meanings of words as they are used in the passage, the key is *as they are used in the passage*. There might be more than one meaning for a word or phrase; you need to look for the option that gives the meaning as it is used in the passage.
- Even if you aren't sure of the meaning of a word, the context should help you select the correct option.
- Look at the following extract, then read through the question and explanation below.

> It was a hot afternoon, and the railway carriage was correspondingly sultry, and the next stop was at Templecombe, nearly an hour ahead. The occupants of the carriage were a small girl, and a smaller girl, and a small boy. An aunt belonging to the children occupied one corner seat, and the further corner seat on the opposite side was occupied by a bachelor who was a stranger to the party, but the small girls and the small boy emphatically occupied the compartment.
>
> From *The Story-Teller* by Saki

Remember

If you are asked about the meaning of a word or phrase in a passage, select the option that gives the meaning of the word or phrase *as it has been used in the text*.

- What is meant by 'the railway carriage was correspondingly sultry'?
  You might not be familiar with the word 'sultry' which means weather that is uncomfortably warm. However, you will most likely be familiar with the word 'correspond' meaning 'match' or 'be similar to'; this should help you understand that the temperature in the carriage matched or was similar to the heat of the afternoon. The context of the events taking place on a 'hot afternoon' makes it clear that the railway carriage is similarly hot.

Synonyms

- A synonym is a word that means the same or virtually the same as another word. For example: *small – little   windy – breezy   start – commence   finish – complete*
- You might be asked to select a word from the answer options that is a synonym for a word in the text.
- Look at this extract, then read the question and explanation.

> Jane's feelings about Martin change when she hears the song he has written for Jo. Before this she thought he was arrogant and insensitive. She realises now that she has misjudged him and from now on treats him with respect.

- Jane originally thinks Martin is 'arrogant and insensitive'. Which option is closest in meaning to these words?

  A humble and kind   **B** conceited and unsympathetic

  C stupid and unworldly   **D** kind and understanding

  The words 'arrogant and insensitive' clearly have a negative meaning; we know this because Jane has 'misjudged' Martin and now she treats him with respect. So, ignore any words that have a positive meaning. Even if you don't know what 'arrogant' means, you know that 'insensitive' is the opposite of 'sensitive' and no other word apart from 'unsympathetic' is similar in meaning. The correct option here is 'conceited and unsympathetic'.

Antonyms

- An antonym is a word that is opposite in meaning to another word. For example: *big – small   rough – smooth   commence – end   heavy – light*
- You might be asked to select a word from the answer options that is an antonym for a word in the text.

> **Remember**
>
> Some words have different meanings, depending on the context in which they are used. If you are asked for an antonym of a word in the text, it will be based on its meaning *in the text*. For example: 'It was a **light** downpour.' A possible antonym of 'light' is **dark**, but in this context, **heavy** would make much more sense.

> **Quick Test**
>
> Read the passage below and then answer the questions.
>
> *Looking back, I see the time we spent on the island as a golden age. It was a time of innocence and great fun. The island was full of fascinating wildlife and larger-than-life characters. We were free to roam and felt that there was adventure waiting around every corner. When the time came to leave, after five wonderful years, I refused to go with my family. I said they could go if they wanted to but I would stay, living off what I could pick or catch and sleeping under the stars. I was nine years old.*
>
> 1. Which word or phrase is closest in meaning to 'innocence' as it is used in the passage?
>
>   **A** not being guilty of any crime   **B** being unaware of the bad things in life
>
>   **C** no responsibilities   **D** freedom
>
> 2. Which word is an antonym of 'larger-than-life'?
>
>   **A** overweight   **B** ordinary   **C** unpleasant   **D** exciting

Author's Intentions and Use of Language Questions

You should be able to:
- identify the effect that the writer wants to create through the use of specific words and phrases.

Understanding the Author's Intentions and Use of Language

- These questions will mainly be about fiction pieces and poems; they ask why the writer might have used specific words and phrases and the effect they wanted to create by describing the characters, setting or atmosphere in a particular way.
- Look out for descriptions that create a particular mood that is in keeping with how characters are feeling or events that are occurring. A boat washed up on a deserted island, for example, will be dramatic and effective if it happens during a storm rather than on an idyllic sunny day!
- Look at the following extract, then read through the questions and explanations below.

Sky Dancers

Hovering, like kestrels, watching avidly for prey,

They flit across the tropical sapphire sky like exotic butterflies,

Nylon strings tugging their twin owners across the salt pans.

Crayoned tails draw sketches in the castle cloud world,

Zigzagging crazily above the water buffalo and bright, upturned faces.

"Watch out, Parvati, it's falling!"

"No it's swooping and diving."

Excited voices in sing-song cadences harmonise in the wind,

Caught in a moment but embedded in the memory for always.

- What effect is created by the highlighted lines?
Hovering, like kestrels, watching avidly for prey: The kites are compared to birds ('kestrels') so that the reader visualises them 'hovering' like large birds looking down from the sky on their prey. This makes them seem alive, not just inanimate objects.
They flit across the tropical sapphire sky like exotic butterflies: Here, the kites are compared to 'exotic butterflies', so not just any old butterflies but brightly coloured, unusual butterflies. The verb 'flit' makes them seem dainty and fast. The sky is

described as 'tropical sapphire' which makes the reader think of sun ('tropical') and a rich blue colour ('sapphire' which is a blue stone/jewel).

Excited voices in sing-song cadences harmonise in the wind: The writer wants to convey a happy mood, describing the kite fliers' voices as being like songs.

- Look at the following extract, then read through the question and explanation below.

Phoebe

As I look at the little statue in the courtyard I remember with affection the day I first saw her. The statue is called Phoebe; she holds a basket of flowers and has bare feet. Now she is covered in lichens that give the stone a lacy covering, but back then she was warm and golden in the summer light. I brush the grey hair from my eyes and remember.

- What effect does the writer want to create about Phoebe by saying 'she was warm and golden in the summer light'?
  The writer wants the statue to appear human (evident from the use of the personal pronoun 'she') and pleasing to look at. The word 'warm' indicates that she is physically warm from the heat of the sun and warm in terms of her personality; 'golden' gives her a precious quality as well as describing the sun on her.

Quick Test

Read this passage and then answer the questions.

Tom and Max heard it take the stairs three at a time then skitter down the tiled hallway towards the kitchen; they followed in hot pursuit. As they reached the bottom of the stairs, the sound of rustling packaging and loud chewing could already be heard from the kitchen. Inside, the boys found a scene of devastation. The floor was littered with spilt flour, pasta and dried fruit, and Barney, the family dog, was cowering under the kitchen table, suspiciously eyeing the sinister creature that was greedily chewing through plastic bags in the corner of the room.

1. What effect is created by the use of the words 'skitter' and 'hot pursuit'?
   A they suggest a sense of calm
   B they suggest a sense of urgency
   C they suggest a sense of horror
   D they suggest that the creature is moving fast

2. Which two words and phrases does the writer use to convey the sounds heard from the kitchen?
   1 rustling   2 skitter   3 loud chewing   4 devastation   5 greedily
   A 1 and 3   B 2 and 4   C 1 and 5   D 3 and 5

Parts of Speech Questions

You should be able to:

- identify nouns, proper nouns and adjectives
- identify pronouns, verbs and adverbs
- identify prepositions and conjunctions.

Identifying Nouns, Proper Nouns and Adjectives

- To answer parts of speech questions, you will need to be able to identify nouns, proper nouns and adjectives.
- A **noun** is a naming word for a person, place, animal or thing (the red words in the text below).
- A **proper noun** is the name of a person or place and begins with a capital letter (the purple words in the text below).
- An **adjective** provides more information about a noun (the green word in the text below):
  Cold soup was delivered to Mrs Hardman in a ward of the Seeland General Hospital.
- A comparative adjective compares one noun with another while a superlative adjective denotes the highest degree.
  - Comparative: *Sally is **heavier** than Kim. Dev is **more intelligent** than Cian.*
  - Superlative: *Glyn is the **most annoying** boy in the class. Cod is my **least favourite** fish.*

> **Remember**
>
> Proper nouns include the names of people, places, days of the week, months of the year and book and film titles.

Identifying Pronouns, Verbs and Adverbs

- Parts of speech questions will also involve identifying pronouns, verbs and adverbs.
- Personal pronouns can either be the subject or the object of a sentence. They can replace a proper noun or noun. For example: *Katya asked **me** if **I** would like to join **her**.*
- Possessive pronouns show ownership. They replace the 'possessor' and the item possessed. For example: *That's not your hat, it's **mine**.*
- Relative pronouns introduce a relative clause, which is a type of subordinate clause. For example: *Our neighbour Ben, **who** helped Mum fix her car, is a mechanic.*
- A verb tells you what the subject of the sentence is doing, being or having (the words in red here): *Fiona swims every morning. Today she is tired as she has a cold, so she is staying at home.*

> **Remember**
>
> **Personal pronouns:** I, you, he, she, it, we, they, me, him, her, us, them
>
> **Possessive pronouns:** mine, yours, his, hers, ours, theirs
>
> **Relative pronouns:** who, which, that, whose, whom

- A verb can also tell you what is being done to the subject: *The book was written by a famous author.*
- An adverb tells you more about the verb (the word in green here): *Markus is running enthusiastically towards the ice-cream van.*
- A fronted adverbial is an adverb or an adverbial phrase (a group of words that functions as an adverb) that comes at the start of a sentence to modify a verb, an adjective, an adverb, a clause or an entire sentence. Fronted adverbials are usually followed by a comma. The words in blue here modify the verb 'walks', telling us *when* Shelley walks her dog.
  Every morning, Shelley walks her dog in the park.

Identifying Prepositions and Conjunctions

- You will also need to be able to identify prepositions and conjunctions.
- Prepositions tell you about when or where something happens.
- Time prepositions help you to understand *when* something happened (the words in blue here):
  at three o'clock   in two months   on Friday
- Place prepositions help you to visualise *where* something happens (the words in green here):
  The mouse ran up the curtain, across the pole and down the wall.
- Conjunctions are words that join two words, phrases or clauses together (the words in red here):
  Kurt packed his waterproof even though it was a hot, sunny day.
  Fiona likes cats and dogs.

> **Remember**
>
> Other examples of **time** (i.e. when) **prepositions** are: next, every, before, between, by, until, since, up to, within.
>
> Other examples of **place** (i.e. where) **prepositions** are: around, behind, below, by, from, into, near, next to, off, on to, outside, towards, under.

> **Quick Test**
>
> Answer these questions about different parts of speech.
>
> 1. Find a proper noun, three nouns and three adjectives in this sentence:
>   Sylvie went shopping and bought some green gloves, some blue tights and a woolly hat.
>
> 2. Identify a pronoun, a verb and an adverb in this sentence:
>   He played quietly on his games console on Saturday morning.
>
> 3. Identify three prepositions and one conjunction in this sentence:
>   The mouse raced across the room, under the piano and into his hole.

Literary Technique Questions

You should be able to:

- identify similes and metaphors
- identify personification
- identify alliteration, onomatopoeia, assonance, repetition and rhyme
- identify hyperbole (exaggeration), irony and rhetorical questions.

Identifying Literary Techniques

- To answer questions about literary techniques, you will need to identify figurative language (which is used to build imagery and create more powerful mental images for the reader).

Similes and Metaphors

- **Similes** create a more vivid description by making comparisons between two nouns.
- The comparisons in a simile are always linked using either 'as' or 'like', so both these words could be clues when looking for similes.
- Similes can be used in texts that are trying to persuade you to agree with a particular point of view or in adverts to persuade you to buy something. For example: *For sale: a beautiful evening dress, as black as night and as soft as a newborn kitten.*
- **Metaphors** compare one thing with another but without using the words 'as' or 'like'. The noun that is being compared to something else is spoken of as if it actually *is* that thing, as opposed to being *like* it.
- To answer these questions, you should look for a person, animal or thing that is being compared to something else as if it actually *is* the thing it is being compared to. For example: *My mum, **an angel** in every other respect, has a tendency to lose her temper if things don't go her way.*

Remember

A handy tip for remembering the difference between similes and metaphors is to remember that there is a letter l in **simile** and also in the word 'like', which is often used when creating a simile.

Personification

- Personification means giving human characteristics to things or ideas. Find the inanimate object that is 'behaving' in a human way. For example: *He was late! The alarm clock shouted at him; the light glared at him. The bed groaned as he got up and the carpet tickled his toes.*

Alliteration

- Alliteration means using words that begin with the same sound and placing them either next to or near each other in a phrase or sentence.
- Look for words that are next to one another or close by that start with the same sound; remember, it is the sound, not the letter, that is the clue. For example:
  - *FUMES FILL FAMILY FLAT*
  - *Stay at Sally's seashore chalet!*

Remember

Alliteration is often used in headlines or adverts to catch the reader's eye.

Onomatopoeia, Assonance, Repetition and Rhyme

- **Onomatopoeia** is when a word sounds like the sound it describes.
- Think about the sound made by each of the following words:
  meow   woof   cluck   baa   crash   bang   wallop
- **Assonance** is when two or more words close together share a similar internal vowel sound.
- Remember, it is the sound (not the letter) that is the clue.
- The following sentence repeats the 'i' sound: *It's dining time for the nine white lions lying by the fire.*
- **Repetition** is often used for emphasis in persuasive speech and writing. For example: *A familiar face, a familiar voice, a familiar emotion…*
- **Rhyme** can help the reader or listener remember what is being said. For example: *A spill, a slip, a hospital trip.*

> **Remember**
>
> Rhyme is often used in slogans and jingles at the end of commercials.

Hyperbole, Irony and Rhetorical Questions

- **Hyperbole** means exaggeration and is a literary technique used to emphasise opinions or feelings.
- It is often used in persuasive writing to drive a point home or to flatter someone so that they might be persuaded to listen to you or take the action you want them to take. For example:
  - *'That building is surely the ugliest and most monstrous ever inflicted on local people.'*
  - *His stomach rumbled like an erupting volcano.*
- **Irony** is saying something that is the opposite of what we actually mean or what would seem appropriate. For example:
  - *Please don't make yourself sick worrying about my health; I just might pull through.*
  - *Ironically, he was run over by the ambulance that came to save him.*
- **Rhetorical questions** are often used in persuasive speech and writing. An answer is not expected. For example: *Do you know how many people have been affected by your lack of consideration?*

> **Quick Test**
>
> 1. Underline the simile in this sentence.
>   The poisonous mushroom looked like a sinister umbrella as it dripped its black blood onto the grass.
>
> 2. Identify the figurative language techniques in these sentences from the list below.
>   onomatopoeia   rhyme   personification   simile
>   a) The curtains blinked and the front door yawned.
>   b) A cough, a sneeze – I've caught a disease!
>   c) The crack of thunder overhead made Danny sprint into the barn.
>   d) The doe was like a beautiful ballerina, leaping gracefully across the fields.

Spelling, Grammar and Punctuation

You should be able to:
- associate the spelling of words to their meaning
- recognise what makes a grammatically correct sentence
- recognise what makes a correctly punctuated sentence.

Spelling

- Some words have letters silent letters, e.g.
  knit   **g**nat   com**b**   castle   **w**rite
- Some words of foreign origin have unusual spellings, e.g.
  scheme   chef   unique   science
- The rule is 'i' before 'e' except after 'c' if the sound is 'ee'. Otherwise, it is usually 'ie' (but there are exceptions), e.g.
  conceive   ceiling   piece   grief   caffeine   seize
- Some words are spelt 'ei' where there is an 'ay' sound, e.g.
  weigh   eight   vein   reign
- **Homophones** are words that sound the same or nearly the same but have different meanings and spellings, e.g.
  air, heir   morning, mourning   to, two, too   there, their, they're
- A **prefix** is a letter or string of letters added to the beginning of a word to turn it into another word. Some prefixes have a negative or opposite meaning, e.g.
  trust – mistrust   perfect – imperfect   load – unload
  legal – illegal   regular – irregular   active – inactive
- A **suffix** is a letter or string of letters added to the end of a word to change its meaning. It can also change the word type, e.g. the suffix -ly can change an adjective into an adverb.

Spelling Plural Words

- The most common plural ending is just adding 's':
  cats   broomsticks   wizards
- When the singular word ends with 'ss', 'ch', 'sh', or 'x', add 'es' to make the plural:
  dresses   kisses   witches   crashes   boxes
- For words ending in 'y', check the letter before the 'y': if the letter is a vowel, just add 's':
  keys   turkeys   valleys
- If the letter before 'y' is a consonant, change the 'y' to an 'i' and add 'es':
  worries   parties   flies
- For some words that end in 'f', change the 'f' to a 'v' and add 'es'. Some of these words can be spelt with 'ves' **and** 'fs':
  elves   halves   hooves/hoofs   scarves/scarfs
- Some words stay the same in the plural:
  sheep   deer   salmon

Remember

Strong spelling, grammar and punctuation skills will help you to answer all kinds of questions quickly and successfully.

Remember

Examples of words with common suffixes include: merri**ly**; injec**tion**; confu**sion**; politi**cian**; ambit**ious**; artif**icial**; part**ial**; observ**ant**; subst**ance**; hesit**ancy**; innoc**ent**; confid**ence**; consist**ency**; ador**able**; notic**eably**; vis**ible**; horri**bly**.

Remember

There are exceptions to these rules. For instance, the plural of fish can be either 'fish' or 'fishes'. Some plurals you just have to learn, including: man – men; woman – women; child – children; tooth – teeth; mouse – mice.

Doubling Letters

- Where a vowel sound is 'short' in a single-syllable word (e.g. sad, pet, pin, spot, run), the consonant following the vowel is doubled before adding the endings -ing, -ed, -er, -est and -y.
- Where a vowel sound is 'long' in words ending in 'e' (e.g. bake, theme, nice, bone, cube), the consonant following the long vowel sound is not doubled and the 'e' at the end of the root word is omitted before adding -ing, -ed, -er, -est and -y.
- When adding -ed, -ence, -al and -ing to words ending in 'fer', the 'r' is doubled if the 'fer' is still stressed after you have added the suffix. For example: refer – referring, referred, referral; infer – inferring, inferred.

Punctuation and Sentence Agreement

- You should know how sentences should be punctuated, including the correct use of capital letters, full stops, speech marks (inverted commas), question marks and exclamation marks.
- These are the main situations in which commas are used:
  - to separate items in a list: *Jo won a glass polar bear, a small teddy, a bear hat and some earmuffs.*
  - to separate adjectives: *The long, sunny days were over.*
  - after a fronted adverbial: *After breakfast, we went out.*
  - to denote an embedded clause: *The cheeky seagull, seeing the huge ice-cream in my hand, quickly snatched it.*
  - to avoid ambiguity: *After we had eaten, Dan the dog wanted to go for a walk.*
- Make sure you can identify the tense of a verb; think about when the action happened (in the past, present or future).
- In longer sentences, the verbs must stay in the appropriate tense, e.g. *Yesterday I **played** in the park, although I **wanted** to go to the match. Today I **am playing** in the park and **paddling** in the pool. Tomorrow I **will play** in the park and **feed** the ducks.*
- If the subject of a sentence is singular, the verb must be too.
  - *Singular:*   Saleem **enjoys** playing computer games.
  - *Plural:*   People **enjoy** playing computer games.

> **Remember**
>
> Capital letters are used for:
> - the first word in a sentence
> - proper nouns such as people's names and place names
> - the start of direct speech
> - first person singular (i.e. 'I').

> **Quick Test**
>
> 1. Insert the missing letters needed to spell each of these words correctly:
>   a) a c c o _ _ _ d a t e   b) e m b a r _ _ _ s m e n t   c) c o n s _ _ _ u s
> 2. Identify any spelling errors in this passage.
>   Melanie was looking forward to a walk with Tim but the forecast was now predicting unsettled weather. Tim said he prefered to wait until later, when hopefully the rain clouds would have passed and there might even be a chance of spoting some sunshine.
> 3. Circle a verb from each pair so that the text makes sense and the verbs agree.
>   Sam **enjoy/enjoys** writing stories because it **gives/given** him the chance to **captures/capture** his ideas in words for other people to **experiences/experience**.

Word Definitions

You should be able to:

- identify the meaning of a word in the context of a given sentence
- use your knowledge of familiar vocabulary to work out the meaning of new words.

Understanding the Meaning of a Word

- The meaning of unfamiliar vocabulary can usually be worked out from the context of the sentence within which it appears.
- Some words have more than one meaning; it depends on the context in which they are used.
- You may be presented with a sentence and asked to choose the meaning of one of the words from a set of five words.

> **Remember**
>
> Think about the word in the context of the sentence. The overall meaning of the sentence is the biggest clue to the word's definition.

> **Example**
>
> Read the sentence below.
>
> **Fergus lolled in the armchair, totally oblivious to the fact that Zena was vacuuming around his feet.**
>
> What does the word 'lolled' mean?
>
> **A** sat upright **B** jumped **C** lazed **D** played **E** flailed

- Consider the meaning of the whole sentence: clearly, Fergus wasn't doing anything active, whereas Zena was vacuuming.
- The word 'lolled' is a verb so should any of the answer options be a different word class, then it can be ruled out.
- The word 'oblivious' tells us that he wasn't conscious of what Zena was doing, which suggests he isn't in a very alert state. Therefore, it is unlikely he was sitting upright, jumping or playing.
- You may not know what the word 'flailed' means. However, 'lazed' *is* a familiar word and fits with the impression the reader gets of Fergus being in a relaxed state.
- Option **C** is the answer.
- You may be given one sentence then asked to define the meaning of **two** different words.

> **Example**
>
> Read the sentence below.
>
> **Petra heard an ominous sound as she opened the cellar door and braced herself for what was to come.**
>
> What does the word 'ominous' mean?
>
> **A** cautious **B** interesting **C** desperation **D** delightful **E** menacing
>
> What does the word 'braced' mean?
>
> **A** frightened **B** prepared **C** persuaded **D** disguised **E** embarrassed

- Establish an understanding of the meaning of the entire sentence first. The phrase 'what was to come' implies that something potentially sinister or dangerous is behind the cellar door.
- The word 'ominous' is an adjective modifying the word 'sound' so 'desperation' can be ruled out because it is a noun.
- Based on the fact that there is something unpleasant behind the door, the meaning is likely to be linked to that. This would rule out 'interesting' and 'delightful'.
- Ask yourself if a sound can be 'cautious'.
- Therefore, the most obvious choice is 'menacing'. Option **E** is the answer.
- In the second sentence, 'braced' is a verb; all the answer options are verbs so they are all potential answers.
- You may have seen or heard the word 'braced' in the context of safety advice on a flight: *should there be a need to protect themselves physically, passengers are advised to 'brace'*. In this context, it is a physical support (by protecting the head with the hands). In this sentence, the implication is that 'braced' indicates a mental preparation for 'what was to come'. It does not make sense for Petra to frighten, persuade, disguise or embarrass herself. Option **B** is the answer.

Odd One Out

You should be able to:

- understand that a word can have multiple meanings
- sort words into possible categories
- identify which words in a set have the strongest link.

Understanding the Multiple Meanings of a Word

- The English language contains lots of words that can have different meanings depending on the context in which they are used.
- Knowing the multiple meanings of as many words as possible will help you with 'odd one out' questions since it will help you to make connections between different words.
- You could be presented with a set of four or five words and asked to find the one which does not fit with the others.

> **Example**
> Four of these words are related in some way. Select the word that does not go with the other four.
>
> **A** field   **B** paddock   **C** meadow   **D** ground   **E** pasture

- Start by thinking about the meanings of the words.
- 'Field' has more than one meaning:
  - It can mean an enclosed, often grassy, area of countryside used for farming.
  - It can mean an area of expertise, e.g. an expert in his field.
  - It can mean an area reserved for a particular activity, for example a sports field or a playing field.
- A 'paddock' is a small field or enclosure where animals are kept.
- 'Meadow' has a similar meaning to 'field'.
- 'Ground' has more than one meaning:
  - It can mean land, or soil.
  - It can mean an area set aside for people to play a game, for example a football ground or a playground.
  - It can be a verb meaning to stop something from leaving.
- 'Pasture' means an area of grassland used for grazing animals.

Sorting Words into Categories

- Think of the ways the words are similar and different:
  - All of the words refer to outside spaces.
  - 'Ground' has more general meanings.
  - 'Ground' and 'field' can both refer to areas set aside for play or sport.
  - 'Field', 'paddock', 'meadow' and 'pasture' are outdoor spaces you might find on a farm.

Remember

You need to look closely at these questions as the connections are often not obvious. Some words have more than one meaning. For example, 'lemon' can be a colour or a fruit.

Identifying the Words with the Strongest Links

- Carefully review the possible groups you have identified.
- There are no other words with a similar meaning to this pair:

field ground	$\longrightarrow$	Words for sporting or play areas

- This is a group of **four** words with a strong link. These words belong together and option **D** ('ground') does not fit with it:

field paddock meadow pasture	$\longrightarrow$	Words for types of farmland

More Difficult Meanings

Example

Three of these words are related in some way. Select the word that does not go with the other three.

A groom   **B** bridle   **C** bridal   **D** stirrup

- There is no obvious theme that fits all of the words.
- Do you understand all of the words?
  - 'Groom' has several meanings.
  - 'Bridle' and 'bridal' are easy to mix up.
  - 'Stirrup' and 'bridle' are unusual words.
- What links can you find between pairs or groups of words?
  - 'Groom' has more than one meaning. It can be a man who is getting married. It could link with 'bridal' because 'bridal' is linked to bride.
  - 'Groom' can also describe someone who takes care of horses. 'Bridle' and 'stirrup' are also words to do with horses, so 'groom', 'bridle' and 'stirrup' could be a group of three.
- Test each of your ideas.
  - Is 'groom' a good match with 'bridal'? There is a link between these two words, but once you remove them, there is no clear link with either of the other two words.
  - Do 'groom', 'bridle', and 'stirrup' make a good group? There is a clear link between these words, which makes 'bridal' the odd one out.
- Option **C** ('bridal') is the odd one out.

Quick Test

In these questions, four of the words are related in some way. Select the word that does not go with the other four.

1. **A** average   **B** typical   **C** normal   **D** constant   **E** ordinary
2. **A** sort   **B** mix   **C** arrange   **D** group   **E** classify

Synonyms and Antonyms

You should be able to:

- find the option that is closest in meaning to a given word
- find the option that is least similar in meaning to a given word.

Synonyms

- Synonyms are words that have similar meanings to each other.
- You could be presented with a given word and be asked to identify the word that is most similar in meaning to it from a list of options.
- The best way to start solving these problems is to understand what types of words you are working with; are they adjectives, nouns, adverbs or verbs?

> **Example**
> Select the word that is most similar in meaning to the following word: shrub
>
> **A** lush   **B** bush   **C** flower   **D** tree   **E** garden

- Identify the type of word you have been given. In the example above, 'shrub' is a noun meaning a type of plant. We are therefore looking for another noun with a similar meaning.
- Looking at the answer options:
  - 'lush' is an adjective that means luxuriant
  - 'bush' is a noun meaning a type of plant
  - 'flower' is a noun meaning a type of plant; it can also be used as a verb meaning to produce flowers or bloom
  - 'tree' is a noun meaning a type of plant
  - 'garden' is a noun meaning a green space around a building; it can also be used as a verb meaning to care for a garden.
- One of 'bush', 'flower' or 'tree' is therefore likely to be the best match.
- If you have more than one possible match, you need to think carefully about the exact meaning of the words to choose the best answer.
- 'Bush', 'flower' and 'tree' are all plants you might find in your garden, so you will need to decide which one is closest in meaning to 'shrub':
- What image comes into your head when you think about a 'shrub'? A shrub tends to be larger than a flower but smaller than a tree, and have a roundish shape.
- Option **B** ('bush') is the best noun that fits and is therefore the correct answer.

Remember

Don't be distracted by words that seem to be linked but are not close in meaning; they are put there to make you think harder!

Antonyms

- Antonyms are words that have opposite meanings to each other.
- You could be presented with a word and be asked to find the word that is least similar in meaning to it from a list of options.
- As with synonyms, the best way to start solving these problems is to understand what types of words you are working with; are they adjectives, nouns, adverbs or verbs?

> **Example**
> Select the word that is least similar in meaning to the following word: heat
>
> **A** lukewarm   **B** melt   **C** cool   **D** boil   **E** freeze

- Identify the type of word you have been given. In the example above, 'heat' can be used as a noun to mean the quality of being hot or it can be used as a verb to mean to become warm or hot.
- Looking at the answer options:
  - 'lukewarm' is an adjective that means moderately warm
  - 'melt' is a verb meaning to turn into liquid (by heat)
  - 'cool' can be an adjective meaning 'fashionable' but it can also be used as a verb meaning to become less hot or as a noun to mean a fairly low temperature
  - 'boil' is a verb meaning to reach the temperature at which a liquid bubbles or starts to turn into vapour
  - 'freeze' is a verb meaning to reach the temperature at which a liquid gets so cold that it turns to a solid (e.g. ice).
- Since we are looking for an antonym, we can quickly rule out 'boil', which has a similar meaning to 'heat'.
- 'Lukewarm' can also be ignored since it is an adjective rather than a noun or a verb.
- 'Melt' is a verb but it involves providing heat to turn something into a liquid, so this option can also be discounted.
- One of 'cool' or 'freeze' is therefore the best match. Think carefully about the exact meaning of the words to choose the best answer.
- The verb 'to freeze' involves reducing the temperature to the extent that liquid particles change to solid particles; 'boil' could therefore be a better antonym for 'freeze'.
- The verb 'to cool' simply refers to a reduction in temperature and therefore this is a better antonym for 'heat', which refers to an increase in temperature.
- Option **C** ('cool') is therefore the correct answer.

> **Remember**
>
> Because some of these comparisons contain quite similar words and ideas, make sure you check all the possible options before deciding on your answer. It is easy to convince yourself that you have found a connection that isn't really there if you don't think the question through properly.

> **Quick Test**
>
> 1. Which of these words is most similar in meaning to the word 'cascade'?
>   **A** splash   **B** damp   **C** waterfall   **D** rinse   **E** staircase
> 2. Which of these words is least similar in meaning to the word 'broad'?
>   **A** narrow   **B** great   **C** wide   **D** thick   **E** large

Word Association

You should be able to:

- use your knowledge of vocabulary and understanding of language to make associations between words
- detect the use of a common expression or idiom.

Associations Between Two Words

- You may be presented with a word and asked to choose the option from a set of five that best corresponds to the word.
- The link between the word and the answer option can be based on a number of factors.
- These types of questions test not only your vocabulary but also your understanding of language, general knowledge, common expressions and idioms.

> **Example**
> Find the word that is most closely associated with the word 'art'.
>
> **A** church **B** gallery **C** school **D** gym **E** library

- Think about the word 'art' and what you would associate it with. You might think of paint, lesson or hobby.
- Now look at the kind of words given in the answer options: they are all buildings/places.
- Ask yourself which one has the most obvious connection with the word 'art'.
- Although you **might** find art in a church, a school, a gym and a library, you would **definitely** find art in a gallery.
- Option **B** is the correct answer.

> **Example**
> Find the word most closely associated with the word 'calf'.
>
> **A** dog **B** lion **C** bear **D** bird **E** camel

- Some questions may test your general knowledge but, even so, there are strategies to help you find the correct answer.
- Think about the word 'calf' in the example above and what you would associate it with. You might know it is the curved part of the back of your leg, between your knee and your foot, but there is nothing like this in the answer options.
- All the answer options are animals. Think about known facts to do with animals, e.g. where they live (den/nest) or the name of an animal's young (puppy/cub). Do any of these animals live in a 'calf'? You may not be sure but don't panic!

Remember

If you have absolutely no idea, move on to the next question. You can always return to the tricky questions when you have finished the test. Then, if you still don't know the answer, have a guess – at least you will have a one-in-five chance of getting it right!

- Now think about their young; you should know that lions and bears have cubs, birds have chicks, dogs have puppies. The word 'calf' may make you think of a young cow but this is not one of the options. You may be aware that the young of other animals are also called 'calves', so by a process of elimination you may be able to work out that a 'calf' is the term used for a young camel.
- Option **E** is the correct answer.

> **Example**
> Find the word most closely associated with the word 'clean'.
>
> **A** shout   **B** speak   **C** trumpet   **D** horn   **E** whistle

- Answers to questions that use common expressions or idioms, like the example above, can be harder to deduce than the other types.
- However, even if you don't know the expression, you may still be able to work out the likely answer by considering the merits of the different options.
- You could associate 'clean' with shouting or speaking, but you are more likely to refer to someone shouting or speaking clearly, rather than 'cleanly'.
- A 'trumpet' and a 'horn' are both instruments that you could blow 'cleanly' into, or produce a clean sound from, but there is little else to separate the two.
- The correct answer is in fact option **E** – the expression 'as clean as a whistle' means very clean or cleanly, as in 'Everything in the kitchen was as clean as a whistle'.

> **Example**
> Find the word most closely associated with the word 'tooth'.
>
> **A** pick   **B** gather   **C** collect   **D** choose   **E** select

- You may be presented with a set of answer options that are synonyms, or near synonyms.
- In the example above, all the words are related in terms of their meaning but clearly one must have an association with a tooth. They are all verbs but the word 'pick' is also a noun.
- A 'toothpick' is a small stick used to remove food from between the teeth.
- Option **A** is the correct answer.

> **Remember**
>
> You may be familiar with idioms such as 'over the moon', 'on cloud nine' and 'as good as gold', but there are a huge number of others in the English language. Again, reading widely or referring to a dictionary of idioms will help you to learn more of them. Do you know these?
>
> - as regular as clockwork
> - as cool as a cucumber
> - at the drop of a hat
> - a bolt from the blue
> - a shot in the dark.

> **Quick Test**
>
> 1. Select the word that is most closely associated with the word 'current'.
>   **A** sultana   **B** raisin   **C** date   **D** grape   **E** electric
> 2. Select the word that is most closely associated with the word 'paint'.
>   **A** waterproof   **B** coat   **C** jacket   **D** blazer   **E** cloak

Cloze

You should be able to:

- understand the context of the sentences or passages that you are asked to read
- choose the correct options to fill in the blanks in each sentence or passage.

What is Cloze?

- Cloze tests consist of sentences or longer passages of writing which have words missing.
- From a set of options, you will need to choose the most suitable word, or words, to fill in the blanks.

Skills for Cloze Questions

- Having good skills in reading comprehension, grammar and punctuation will help you to identify the correct answers in cloze questions. Having a wide range of vocabulary will also help you.
- When choosing the most suitable word (or words) to fill a space, you need to ensure that it is punctuated appropriately and maintains agreement in the sentence (this includes ensuring that the verbs and pronouns work consistently).

Approaching the Questions

- First read the whole sentence in order to get an understanding of its context.

Example

Complete the sentence in the most sensible way by selecting the appropriate combination of words from within the brackets. Use one word from each set of brackets.

(Since, After, However) years and years of taking driving lessons, not to mention three (failed, missing, successful) attempts, Nico finally passed his driving test.

A Since, failed   **B** Since, missing   **C** After, failed   **D** After, successful   **E** However, missing

- Reading the sentence, the words 'finally passed' indicate that Nico has been trying to succeed for some time.
- In the first bracket, 'Since' and 'However' wouldn't be suitable ways of starting the sentence but 'After' fits perfectly.
- We can now focus on options **C** and **D** only, which both offer adjectives ('failed' and 'successful') that could potentially fit with the noun 'attempts'.
- However, the fact that Nico has 'finally passed' means that he can't have been 'successful' before so 'failed' would be the more suitable option. So **C** is the correct answer.

- You may be given a passage in which whole sentences or parts of sentences are missing.

Example

In this passage, some of the words are missing. Complete the passage by selecting the best set of words for each question.

In summer, a country squire's hour of rising was often four o'clock **[Question 1]** after which his labourers went to their work and he to his. At twelve, he would dine together with his household: **[Question 2]** In the afternoon, the squire rode about his farms watching over his tenants and seeing that the fences were in good repair and the roads well kept. **[Question 3]** It was his duty to know everything and everybody; if any parent brought up his child in idleness, it was his responsibility to interfere and see that the child was taught an honest trade; if any youths took to gaming or frequenting inns or taverns, he would see that they were **[Question 4]** such as archery so that they might be useful soldiers in times of need.

A good beef, mutton, vegetables and ale.

B instead taught manly exercises and skills

C robbers and brigands could be summarily hung from the nearest tree

D with breakfast at five,

E The country squire in those days was also the local magistrate.

- Read the extract to get a sense of what it is about.
- Look for words or phrases which might indicate the sequence or progression of events and actions, e.g. words to do with time or place.
- Look at the possible answers to get a sense of where they might fit in the passage.
- Pay close attention to the punctuation both in the possible answers and around the gaps in the passage. For example, if there is a full stop before a gap, then look for an answer that starts with a capital letter; if there is a colon before a gap, it may indicate that it should be followed by a list.
- The answers for the passage above are:
  Question 1. **D**; Question 2. **A**; Question 3. **E**; Question 4. **B**

Remember

If time allows, read the passage again with your answers in place to see if the sentences flow and make sense.

Quick Test

Read the passage and select the most appropriate word from the options to complete each question.

A banks   B built   C cities   D divided   E parks
F fascinating   G families   H torn   I culture   J travelling

Berlin is the capital of Germany and one of the largest **[Question 1]** in Europe. It is located in the northeast of the country, close to the border with Poland. Lying on the **[Question 2]** of the River Spree, it has a population of approximately 3.6 million.

Berlin has a temperate climate and is full of forests, **[Question 3]**, gardens and lakes. Locals love to spend warm summer evenings and weekends relaxing in the parks with their friends and family. The city prides itself on its emphasis on **[Question 4]** and it is home to many museums and opera houses. The recent history of the city is **[Question 5]** and unique. Throughout the 1970s and 1980s, a wall **[Question 6]** the eastern and western parts of the city. This partition was **[Question 7]** almost overnight and **[Question 8]** from the east to the west of the city was forbidden. Therefore, many **[Question 9]** were separated for decades, only to be reunited when the wall was **[Question 10]** down in 1989.

Shuffled Sentences

You should be able to:

- unravel sentences where the words have been shuffled
- identify one word in each sentence that is unnecessary.

Skills for Unravelling Shuffled Sentences

- Try to identify the subject from the words in the shuffled sentence.
- See if you can pair the subject with a verb.
- Ask yourself if there is an adjective that modifies the subject or an adverb that modifies the verb.
- Once you have grouped some elements, you should be able to form a sentence that makes sense and identify the 'rogue' or unnecessary word.
- This word is the answer you will pick from the five answer options.
- The shuffled sentence could contain homophones which will test your spelling skills.

Remember

Not all the words from the shuffled sentence will appear in the given answer options.

Example

Rearrange the sentence correctly in order to identify the unnecessary word.

eats breakfast sister my cereal for have

A have **B** cereal **C** breakfast **D** sister **E** eats

- First, identify the subject of the sentence; then you will be able to find the verb by asking yourself what the person or thing is doing.
- There is reference to a 'sister' who could be the subject; there are two verbs – 'eats' and 'have'. The word 'sister' is singular and the only verb that agrees with this is 'eats'; 'have' does not agree with 'cereal' or 'breakfast' either and as they are inanimate objects, the verb 'eats' does not make sense with them.
- You will now be able to unshuffle the sentence so that it is *My sister eats cereal for breakfast.* and thus establish that 'have' is the unnecessary word.
- Option **A** is the correct answer.

Remember

You may be able to quickly identify the word that doesn't fit with the context of the others without spending time unravelling the whole sentence.

> **Quick Test**
>
> Rearrange the sentences correctly in order to identify the unnecessary word in each.
>
> 1. a window of the necklace in Max threw kitchen the out through rage
>
>   A window B threw C kitchen D through E rage
>
> 2. had to believe sales job was been the tougher impression than Brogan led
>
>   A led B impression C tougher D believe E sales

Collins

11+
Verbal Reasoning

Practice

Workbook

YOU HAVE 10 QUESTIONS TO COMPLETE WITHIN THE TIME GIVEN.

South Africa is becoming an increasingly popular holiday destination. People from all over the world are being attracted by its natural beauty, cosmopolitan cities and diverse wildlife. Cape Town, the capital of South Africa, is especially popular. The city is dynamic and exciting and has a rich history and culture. It is also home to the stunning Table Mountain, which you can ascend on foot or by cable car.

Example i

Which of the following is not mentioned as a reason why people are attracted to South Africa?
A   Natural beauty
B   Excellent food
C   Cosmopolitan cities
D   Diverse wildlife

The correct answer is **B**. This has already been marked in Example i in Practice Test 1 of your answer sheet on page 153.

Example ii

What is the name of the mountain in Cape Town?
A   Cape Mountain
B   Africa Mountain
C   Table Mountain
D   Leopard Mountain

The correct answer is **C**. Mark the answer C in Example ii in Practice Test 1 of your answer sheet on page 153.

Read the passage below and then answer the questions that follow.

An extract from: *The Limpopo Academy of Private Detection*

by Alexander McCall-Smith

In Botswana, home to the No. 1 Ladies Detective Agency for the problems of ladies, and others, it is customary – one might say very customary – to enquire of the people whom you meet whether they have slept well. The answer to that question is almost inevitably that they have indeed slept well, even if they have not, and have spent the night tossing and turning as a result of the nocturnal barking of dogs, the activity of mosquitoes or the prickings of a bad conscience. Of course, mosquitoes may be defeated by nets or sprays, just as dogs may be roundly scolded; a bad conscience, though, is not so easily stifled. If somebody were to invent a spray capable of dealing with an uncomfortable conscience, that person would undoubtedly do rather well – but perhaps might not sleep as soundly as before, were he to reflect on the consequences of his invention. Bad consciences, it would appear, are there for a purpose: to make us feel regret over our failings. Should they be silenced, then our entirely human weaknesses, our manifold omissions, would become all the greater – and that, as Mma Ramotswe would certainly say, is not a good thing.

Mma Ramotswe was fortunate in having an untroubled conscience, and therefore generally enjoyed undisturbed sleep. It was her habit to take to her bed after a final cup of red bush tea at around ten o'clock at night. Mr. J.L.B. Matekoni, her husband and by common consent the finest mechanic in all Botswana, would often retire before her, particularly if he had had a tiring day at work. Mechanics in general sleep well, as do many others whose day is taken up with physically demanding labour. So by the time that Mma Ramotswe went to bed, he might already be lost to this world, his breathing deep and regular, his eyes firmly closed to the bedside light that he would leave for his wife to extinguish.

She would not take long to go to sleep, drifting off to thoughts of what had happened that day; to images of herself drinking tea in the office or driving her van on an errand; to the picture of Mma Makutsi sitting upright at her desk, her large glasses catching the light as she held forth on some issue or other. Or to some memory of a long time ago, of her father walking down a dusty road, holding her hand and explaining to her about the ways of cattle – a subject that he knew so well. When a wise man dies, there is so much history that is lost: that is what they said, and Mma Ramotswe knew it to be true. Her own father, the late Obed Ramotswe, had taken so much with him, but had also left much behind, so many memories and sayings and observations, that she, his daughter, could now call up and cherish as she waited for the soft arms of sleep to embrace her.

1 In which country does this story take place?

A Botswana

B Nigeria

C Africa

D Morocco

2 According to the passage, which of the following questions is it usual to be asked?

A 'What did you eat?'

B 'How are your parents?'

C 'Did you sleep well?'

D 'How old are you?'

3 According to the passage, what is an effective way of dealing with mosquitoes?

A Dousing them with buckets of water

B Shooting them

C Using sprays or nets

D Befriending them

4 What is the purpose of a 'bad conscience'?

A To ensure that our successes are not forgotten

B To make us feel depressed

C To cause us pain

D To remind us to be remorseful for our mistakes

5 At what time did Mma Ramotswe drink her tea?

A 10 p.m.

B 3 p.m.

C 2:30 p.m.

D 11:30 p.m.

6 According to the passage, why do mechanics sleep well?

A Because they are often lazy

B Because they are tired from a hard day's work

C Because they drink lots of tea

D Because they go to bed very late

7 **What did Mma Ramotswe think about before falling asleep?**

Option 1: mechanical work that needed to be completed

Option 2: Mma Makutsi sitting at her desk

Option 3: drinking tea at home

Option 4: driving her vehicle

A Options 1 and 3 only

B Options 2 and 4 only

C Options 1, 2 and 4 only

D All of the above

8 **On which of the following subjects was Obed Ramotswe knowledgeable?**

A How to repair a car

B How to tend to cows

C How to run a law firm

D How to deal with intruders

9 **What does the word 'extinguish' mean?**

A Detest

B Protect

C Smell

D Quench

10 **What was Mma Ramotswe's relationship with her late father like?**

A They hated each other

B They never met

C They were unhappy

D They were close

END OF TEST

YOU HAVE 10 QUESTIONS TO COMPLETE WITHIN THE TIME GIVEN.

South Africa is becoming an increasingly popular holiday destination. People from all over the world are being attracted by its natural beauty, cosmopolitan cities and diverse wildlife. Cape Town, the capital of South Africa, is especially popular. The city is dynamic and exciting and has a rich history and culture. It is also home to the stunning Table Mountain, which you can ascend on foot or by cable car.

Example i

Which of the following is not mentioned as a reason why people are attracted to South Africa?

A Natural beauty

B Excellent food

C Cosmopolitan cities

D Diverse wildlife

The correct answer is **B**. This has already been marked in Example i in Practice Test 2 of your answer sheet on page 153.

Example ii

What is the name of the mountain in Cape Town?

A Cape Mountain

B Africa Mountain

C Table Mountain

D Leopard Mountain

The correct answer is **C**. Mark the answer C in Example ii in Practice Test 2 of your answer sheet on page 153.

Read the passage below and then answer the questions that follow.

An extract from: *Wicked*

by Gregory Maguire

"Storm on the horizon," said the Scarecrow. Miles off, thunder echoed. "There-is-a-Witch on the horizon," said the Tin Woodman, tickling the Lion. The Lion got spooked and rolled on top of the Scarecrow, whimpering, and the Tin Woodman collapsed on top of them both.

"Good friends, should we be wary of that storm?" said the girl. The rising winds moved the curtain of greenery at last, and the Witch caught sight of the girl. She was sitting with her feet tucked underneath her and her arms wrapped around her knees. She was not a dainty thing but a good-size farm girl, dressed in blue-and-white checks and a pinafore. In her lap, a vile little dog cowered and whined.

"The storm makes you skittish. It's natural after what you've been through," said the Tin Woodman. "Relax."

The Witch's fingers dug into the bark of the tree. She still could not see the girl's face, just her strong forearms and the crown of her head where her dark hair was pulled back into pigtails. Was she to be taken seriously, or was she merely a blow-away dandelion seed, caught on the wrong side of the wind? If she could see the girl's face, the Witch felt she might know. But as the Witch craned outward from the trunk, the girl at the same time twisted her face, turning away.

"That storm is coming closer, and in a hurry." The feeling in her voice rose as the wind rose. She had a throaty vehemence, like someone arguing through the threat of impending tears. "I know storms, I know how they come upon you!"

"We're safer here," said the Tin Woodman.

"Certainly we are not," answered the girl, "because this tree is the highest point around, and if lightning is to strike, it will strike here." She clutched her dog. "Didn't we see a shed farther up the road? Come, come; Scarecrow, if there's lightning, you'll burn the fastest! Come on!"

She was up and running in an ungainly way, and her companions followed in a mounting panic. As the first hard drops of rain fell, the Witch caught sight, not of the girl's face, but of the shoes. Her sister's shoes. They sparkled even in the darkening afternoon. They sparkled like yellow diamonds, and embers of blood, and thorny stars.

If she had seen the shoes first, the Witch would never have been able to listen to the girl or her friends. But the girl's legs had been tucked beneath her skirt. Now the Witch was reminded of her need. The shoes should be hers! Hadn't she endured enough, hadn't she earned them? The Witch would fall on the girl from the sky, and wrestle those shoes off her impertinent feet, if only she could.

But the storm from which the companions raced, farther and faster along the Yellow Brick Road, troubled the Witch more than it did the girl who had gone through rain and the Scarecrow whom lightning could burn. The Witch could not venture out in such a vicious, insinuating wetness.

Instead, she had to tuck herself between some exposed roots of the black willow tree, where no water could endanger her, and wait for the storm to pass.

She would emerge. She always had before. The punishing political climate of Oz had beat her down, dried her up, tossed her away – like a seedling she had drifted, apparently too desiccated ever to take root. But surely the curse was on the land of Oz, not on her. Though Oz had given her a twisted life, hadn't it also made her capable? No matter that the companions had hurried away. The Witch could wait. They would meet again.

1 **What was the girl doing when first seen by the Witch?**

   A The girl was running

   B The girl was eating

   C The girl was crying

   D The girl was sitting

2 **Which word best describes the girl's physical appearance?**

   A Skinny

   B Obese

   C Slim

   D Robust

3 **According to the Tin Woodman, how did the girl feel about the storm?**

   A Nervous

   B Prepared

   C Indifferent

   D Relaxed

4 **Why did the Witch want to see the girl's face?**

   A The Witch wanted to see if she could recognise the girl

   B The Witch thought it would help her get the measure of the girl

   C The Witch had heard that the girl was very beautiful

   D The Witch wanted to take a picture of the girl's face

5   **Which word best describes how the girl ran?**

    A Clumsily

    B Powerfully

    C Correctly

    D Elegantly

6   **Which literary technique is used in this phrase: 'They sparkled like yellow diamonds…' ?**

    A Metaphor

    B Alliteration

    C Simile

    D Personification

7   **Why did the Witch not chase the girl immediately?**

    A She was tired from her earlier exertions

    B The girl was running too fast

    C She could not venture out in the rain

    D She had no interest in chasing the girl

8   **How had the Witch fared in the land of Oz?**

    A She had thrived and prospered

    B She had faced many obstacles and setbacks

    C She had avoided any difficulties

    D She had been treated well by all

9   **What does the word 'impending' mean?**

    A Pendulum

    B Imminent

    C Impatient

    D Imploring

10   **Which of the following is the best antonym of 'mounting'?**

    A Riding

    B Decreasing

    C Melting

    D Rising

END OF TEST

YOU HAVE 10 QUESTIONS TO COMPLETE WITHIN THE TIME GIVEN.

Some people choose to start their Christmas shopping early in October. It has been reported that some people even buy their Christmas presents in the sales in August. In recent years, people have had the option of purchasing their Christmas presents online.

Example i

According to the passage, what is the earliest that people start their Christmas shopping?

A In the preceding summer

B In the preceding October

C Christmas Eve

D In early December

The correct answer is **A**. This has already been marked in Example i in Practice Test 3 of your answer sheet on page 153.

Example ii

In recent years, what has caused a change in how people shop?

A There are more shops.

B Shops are more crowded.

C New products are available.

D There has been a rise in use of the internet.

The correct answer is **D**. Mark the answer D in Example ii in Practice Test 3 of your answer sheet on page 153.

Read the passage below and then answer the questions that follow.

The World of Journalism

Investigative journalists are responsible for writing in-depth news stories; these can be about anything and everything, but often focus on politics, social issues and crime. Writing a newsworthy story involves a lot of hard work: research, investigation, verifying facts and forming relationships with sources and eye-witnesses in order to get the most out of interviewing them. Media stories can be delivered to the public through magazines and newspapers, broadcast media or internet platforms.

A successful journalist will have excellent written and verbal communication skills and be curious and impartial. An editor checks the journalist's work before it goes to print or on air, ensuring that the language is clear and the facts are accurate. News reports are supposed to be objective: in other words, the journalist is not meant to take a particular side. However, this isn't always the case!

Some news stories, for example where a family member has been injured or killed, are distressing so journalists need to be considerate of the emotions of the contacts they interview for their report.

One important role of a journalist is holding public figures to account. In other words, questioning people, such as politicians, about their actions and presenting their findings to the general public. They also play a part in raising the profile of community issues and charitable causes, for example local fundraisers and national events like Children in Need.

Paparazzi

Paparazzi are independent photographers – they work for themselves. They take pictures of celebrities and public figures such as actors, politicians, royalty and performers without their permission, and usually while these people are 'off-guard', going about their daily routines. Once a celebrity is in the limelight, the paparazzi swarm like flies to get the shot they hope will make them as rich and famous as their target! The photographs are then sold to various media outlets such as gossip magazines and the tabloid press. These pictures are then easily displayed on social media where they are shared throughout the world.

Paparazzi are unpopular as they invade their subjects' privacy. Sometimes, their behaviour is classed as stalking which is a criminal offence. The most famous incidence of this was when a car carrying the Princess of Wales tried to escape pursuing paparazzi in Paris in 1997. The car crashed during the chase, resulting in her death.

1 According to the passage, which topics are frequently covered in a news story?

   A research, social issues and sources

   B politics, social issues and crime

   C politics, facts and eye-witnesses

   D crime, sources and relationships

2 What can an investigative journalist do to get a good story when interviewing a source?

   A Offer the source money

   B Work really hard

   C Build a relationship with the source

   D Stalk the source

3 Why do you think that being curious helps to make a journalist successful?

   A They need to be eager to find out things.

   B They need to be impartial.

   C They need to have excellent verbal communication skills.

   D They need to check their work.

4 Why should journalists be mindful of the emotions of their contacts?

   A So that the report is clear and accurate.

   B To enable the editor to check their work.

   C So that the news report is objective.

   D In case the story they are covering is distressing.

5 To whom do the paparazzi sell their photographs?

   A Media organisations

   B Public figures

   C Members of the royal family

   D Celebrities

6 According to the passage, why might the paparazzi have a poor reputation?

   A They charge a lot for their photographs.

   B They harass their subjects.

   C They don't check their work.

   D They sell their work to the tabloid press.

7 What is the meaning of the word 'off-guard' as used in the passage?

A unaffected

B off duty

C unprepared

D busy

8 What is the name of the literary technique used to describe the paparazzi in the sentence extract below?

…the paparazzi swarm like flies…

A Metaphor

B Alliteration

C Personification

D Simile

9 Which word is used in the passage to describe 'harassment'?

A criminal

B stalking

C offence

D behaviour

10 Which word means the same as 'pursuing' as used in the last paragraph?

A keen

B criminal

C offending

D following

END OF TEST

YOU HAVE 10 QUESTIONS TO COMPLETE WITHIN THE TIME GIVEN.

Some people choose to start their Christmas shopping early in October. It has been reported that some people even buy their Christmas presents in the sales in August. In recent years, people have had the option of purchasing their Christmas presents online.

Example i

According to the passage, what is the earliest that people start their Christmas shopping?

A   In the preceding summer

B   In the preceding October

C   Christmas Eve

D   In early December

The correct answer is **A**. This has already been marked in Example i in Practice Test 4 of your answer sheet on page 153.

Example ii

In recent years, what has caused a change in how people shop?

A   There are more shops.

B   Shops are more crowded.

C   New products are available.

D   There has been a rise in use of the internet.

The correct answer is **D**. Mark the answer D in Example ii in Practice Test 4 of your answer sheet on page 153.

Read the passage below and then answer the questions that follow.

The Vikings

Who were the Vikings? The Vikings, or Norse, were Scandinavian warriors who attacked Northern Europe, Eastern Asia and Eastern North America.

Between 860 and 960 AD, the Norwegian Vikings invaded then traded with their neighbours to the west, Iceland and Greenland. The Swedish Vikings set out across the Baltic Sea into Northern Europe, raiding, then buying and selling before finally settling. By the end of the first millennium, the Vikings, in their open longboats, had reached North America, five hundred years before Columbus. The word 'Viking' means one who lurks in a 'Vik' or bay: the Vikings were skilful in lying in wait before taking unsuspecting coastal villages by surprise, like sharks circling for the kill.

How do we know about the Vikings? Archaeology provides physical information about their daily lives, where they settled and what these settlements looked like.

The large number of horn artefacts found in Viking settlements led to a Tudor historian suggesting that Vikings wore horned helmets; yet any Viking warrior would have known that horns on a helmet just made it easier for their opponent to grab hold of them in close battle. There is some evidence that hats with antlers were used in religious ceremonies. Plutarch, writing in the first century AD, describes Northern Europeans as dressing up with head-dresses that resemble wild beasts, and a ninth-century tapestry in Oseberg, Norway, shows a man wearing a set of horns.

Written records about the Vikings were almost all created by priests. The Vikings were considered heathens* for their attacks on monasteries and, as a result, were portrayed in the worst possible way.

What did the Vikings want to achieve? One of the main reasons for the Vikings' early raiding and trading missions was to obtain food to take back home where there were limited sources of food. They also wanted to create settlements in the fertile farmlands of their foes. Unlike many other invaders and settlers, they were not trying to spread their pagan religion but were keen to find out about the social and technological advances that they observed in Britain and southern European countries.

Did the Vikings deserve their reputation for aggression and brutality? As the only written records are likely to be biased, and there are also many examples of Vikings trading and settling, it is possible that the Vikings were not quite the vicious villains they have been portrayed as. They brought valuable commodities such as honey, tin, wheat, wool, wood, iron, fur, leather, fish and walrus ivory with them and helped build up the farming communities of southern England. So maybe the Vikings weren't quite as bad as history suggests.

*heathen: someone who does not believe in God

1 Which two places were the western neighbours to the Viking homelands?

Option 1: Iceland

Option 2: Eastern North America

Option 3: Russia

Option 4: Greenland

A Options 1 and 3

B Options 1 and 4

C Options 2 and 3

D Options 2 and 4

2 Which area of water did the Swedish Vikings cross when they started raiding?

A North Sea

B Atlantic Ocean

C English Channel

D Baltic Sea

3 What is the fourth paragraph mainly about?

A Viking warriors

B Viking farming

C Viking head-dresses

D Viking gods

4 Which two pieces of evidence tell us that the Vikings could have had hats with horns?

Option 1: a Norwegian tapestry

Option 2: a cave painting

Option 3: a priest's diary

Option 4: Plutarch's writings

A Options 1 and 4

B Options 1 and 3

C Options 2 and 3

D Options 2 and 4

5   **Why do you think the written records about Vikings might have been biased?**

    A   There were no printing machines in those days.

    B   The priests who wrote them didn't like the fact that they were heathens.

    C   The priests were jealous of the Vikings.

    D   The records have been rewritten repeatedly and changed over time.

6   **How were the Vikings different from other invaders and settlers?**

    A   They sailed in longboats.

    B   They didn't try to spread their religion.

    C   They were pagan.

    D   They wore horned helmets.

7   **Which of these words is closest in meaning to 'commodities' as it is used in paragraph seven?**

    A   food

    B   gemstones

    C   products

    D   tapestries

8   **Why might the Vikings not have been quite as bad as history suggests?**

    A   They brought valuable commodities and helped build up farming communities.

    B   They introduced their pagan religion to the areas they raided.

    C   There are tapestries showing them making friends with farming communities.

    D   Columbus admired their technological advances.

9   **What type of words are these?**

coastal   horned   religious   fertile

    A   adverbs

    B   adjectives

    C   prepositions

    D   nouns

10   **Choose another suitable heading for the final paragraph.**

    A   How long ago did the Vikings live?

    B   Viking daily life

    C   The Viking – friend or foe?

    D   Viking settlements

END OF TEST

YOU HAVE 16 QUESTIONS TO COMPLETE WITHIN THE TIME GIVEN.

Example i

Identify a homophone of the word 'night' from the words below.

A	B	C	D	E
knight	dark	bright	summer	light

The correct answer is **A**. This has already been marked in Example i in Practice Test 5 of your answer sheet on page 154.

Example ii

Select the correct prefix to give the opposite of the word 'believable'.

A	B	C	D	E
in	un	on	mis	pro

The correct answer is **B**. Mark the answer B in Example ii in Practice Test 5 of your answer sheet on page 154.

1 Identify a homophone of the word 'faint' from the words below.

A	B	C	D	E
fine	feint	recover	swoon	feign

2 Identify a homophone of the word 'straight' from the words below.

A	B	C	D	E
direct	strut	stray	strait	street

3 What type of word is 'slowly'?

A	B	C	D	E
adjective	verb	pronoun	adverb	noun

4 What type of word is 'her'?

A	B	C	D	E
preposition	verb	pronoun	adverb	noun

5 Select the correct prefix to give the opposite of the word 'agreeable'.

A	B	C	D	E
up	dis	un	in	mis

6 Select the correct prefix to give the opposite of the word 'treat'.

A	B	C	D	E
up	dis	un	in	mis

7 Select the word below that is misspelt.

A	B	C	D	E
curiosity	thorough	different	rythym	mischievous

8 Select the word below that is misspelt.

A	B	C	D	E
hollow	desparate	smartly	definite	twelfth

9 Select the word below that is misspelt.

A	B	C	D	E
harass	handy	calender	suffocate	describe

10 Select the word below that is misspelt.

A	B	C	D	E
timid	greatful	singular	guarantee	tremor

11 Select the word below that is misspelt.

A	B	C	D	E
seperate	injured	politely	beseech	exaggerate

12 Complete this word correctly by inserting the missing letters.

i m m _ _ _ a t e l y

13 Complete this word correctly by inserting the missing letters.

d i s a _ _ _ o u s

14 Complete this word correctly by inserting the missing letters.

i n t _ _ _ u p t

15 Complete this word correctly by inserting the missing letters.

g o v _ _ _ m e n t

16 Complete this word correctly by inserting the missing letters.

h i n _ _ _ n c e

END OF TEST

YOU HAVE 15 QUESTIONS TO COMPLETE WITHIN THE TIME GIVEN.

Example i

Select the word that is most similar in meaning to the following word:

push

A	B	C	D	E
shallow	shove	tug	hollow	cry

The correct answer is **B**. This has already been marked in Example i in Practice Test 6 of your answer sheet on page 154.

Example ii

Select the word that is most similar in meaning to the following word:

imitate

A	B	C	D	E
cover	copy	grow	live	irritate

The correct answer is **B**. Mark the answer B in Example ii in Practice Test 6 of your answer sheet on page 154.

For each row, select the word from the table that is most similar in meaning to the given word.

1 allow

A	B	C	D	E
forbid	aloud	permit	drive	made

2 blank

A	B	C	D	E
blink	preserve	full	admit	empty

3 cunning

A	B	C	D	E
swimming	clever	evil	foolish	cold

4 false

A	B	C	D	E
frozen	falter	feign	untrue	dislike

5 glad

A	B	C	D	E
happy	injure	give	upset	gown

6 huge

A	B	C	D	E
high	miniscule	undue	mortify	enormous

7 loyal

A	B	C	D	E
leave	dishonest	faithful	fortitude	lawn

8 rowdy

A	B	C	D	E
timid	fortunate	shrouded	noisy	rouse

9 polite

A	B	C	D	E
politician	holy	rude	aggressive	courteous

10 rare

A	B	C	D	E
royal	scarce	mercy	steak	abundant

11 real

A	B	C	D	E
reel	arson	duplicate	genuine	phoney

12 abandon

A	B	C	D	E
alert	home	call	leave	remain

13 rich

A	B	C	D	E
pauper	clothes	wealthy	house	money

14 rude

A	B	C	D	E
gentle	impolite	commerce	prude	argue

15 safe

A	B	C	D	E
sail	protect	dangerous	damage	secure

END OF TEST

YOU HAVE 15 QUESTIONS TO COMPLETE WITHIN THE TIME GIVEN.

Example i

Select the word that is most opposite in meaning to the following word:

hot

A	B	C	D	E
follow	cold	freeze	ice	jelly

The correct answer is **B**. This has already been marked in Example i in Practice Test 7 of your answer sheet on page 154.

Example ii

Select the word that is most opposite in meaning to the following word:

below

A	B	C	D	E
attack	deep	lower	above	before

The correct answer is **D**. Mark the answer D in Example ii in Practice Test 7 of your answer sheet on page 154.

For each row, select the word from the table that is most opposite in meaning to the given word.

1 after

A	B	C	D	E
later	summer	night	before	how

2 handsome

A	B	C	D	E
beautiful	soldier	ugly	simmer	pretty

3 winner

A	B	C	D	E
gold	loser	practice	first	shake

4 insult

A	B	C	D	E
salty	foreign	attack	compliment	shine

5 allow

A	B	C	D	E
aloud	hover	permit	grant	forbid

6 lack

A	B	C	D	E
back	leisure	lesson	abundance	drought

7 junior

A	B	C	D	E
young	jealous	parasite	doctor	senior

8 kind

A	B	C	D	E
cruel	closed	clever	clear	conscious

9 narrow

A	B	C	D	E
deep	broad	tight	river	thin

10 always

A	B	C	D	E
often	hindrance	never	heighten	almost

11 simple

A	B	C	D	E
fraught	complicated	pine	simply	police

12 careful

A	B	C	D	E
hateful	caring	mindful	careless	protective

13 general

A	B	C	D	E
gesture	horse	particular	cavalry	army

14 peace

A	B	C	D	E
piece	harmony	tranquil	agitate	war

15 artificial

A	B	C	D	E
art	mountain	natural	sky	powerful

END OF TEST

Definitions

5 mins

YOU HAVE 16 QUESTIONS TO COMPLETE WITHIN THE TIME GIVEN.

Read the sentences and select the most appropriate word to answer each question.

Example i

The squirrel hurried to gather acorns before concealing the hoard in a hollow tree.

What does the word 'concealing' mean?

A	B	C	D	E
covering	leaving	hiding	eating	placing

The correct answer is **C**. This has already been marked in Example i in Practice Test 8 of your answer sheet on page 154.

What does the word 'hoard' mean?

A	B	C	D	E
food	collection	rest	treasure	bag

The correct answer is **B**. This has already been marked in Example i in Practice Test 8 of your answer sheet on page 154.

Example ii

The king seemed content with the gifts he had received from his subjects.

What does the word 'content' mean?

A	B	C	D	E
unhappy	annoyed	worried	excited	pleased

The correct answer is **E**. Mark the answer E in Example ii in Practice Test 8 of your answer sheet on page 154.

What does the word 'subjects' mean?

A	B	C	D	E
people	teacher	soldiers	family	lands

The correct answer is **A**. Mark the answer A in Example ii in Practice Test 8 of your answer sheet on page 154.

Read the sentences and select the most appropriate word to answer each question.

Tom decided what to purchase and stepped purposefully into the interior of the shop.

1 What does the word 'purchase' mean?

A	B	C	D	E
choose	afford	buy	spend	request

2 What does the word 'interior' mean?

A	B	C	D	E
inside	doorway	entrance	space	cellar

The firefighter displayed a lot of courage when he entered the burning building and hauled the man to safety.

3 What does the word 'courage' mean?

A	B	C	D	E
anger	fear	patience	hope	bravery

4 What does the word 'hauled' mean?

A	B	C	D	E
took	helped	pushed	pulled	threw

Fortunately, the room was vacant and the furnishings were quite lavish.

5 What does the word 'vacant' mean?

A	B	C	D	E
unoccupied	open	large	tidy	airy

6 What does the word 'lavish' mean?

A	B	C	D	E
colourful	luxurious	comfortable	practical	basic

The wrestler's face contorted in pain but he was determined not to yield to his opponent.

7 What does the word 'contorted' mean?

A	B	C	D	E
grunted	shook	rocked	sweated	twisted

8 What does the word 'yield' mean?

A	B	C	D	E
shout	surrender	yell	rush	smile

The meeting promptly approved the financial policy.

9 What does the word 'promptly' mean?

A	B	C	D	E
immediately	finally	carefully	always	actually

10 What does the word 'approved' mean?

A	B	C	D	E
tested	rejected	agreed	altered	completed

The policeman warned the motorist to proceed with caution.

11 What does the word 'proceed' mean?

A	B	C	D	E
stop	continue	start	turn	speed

12 What does the word 'caution' mean?

A	B	C	D	E
confidence	intention	fear	licence	care

The team manager rebuked the players for missing many opportunities to score.

13 What does the word 'rebuked' mean?

A	B	C	D	E
praised	shamed	criticised	thanked	teased

14 What does the word 'opportunities' mean?

A	B	C	D	E
kicks	shots	attempts	chances	turns

The pupil stood tongue-tied before the headmaster who glowered at him over the top of his glasses.

15 What does the word 'tongue-tied' mean?

A	B	C	D	E
nervously	afraid	speechless	cheekily	bravely

16 What does the word 'glowered' mean?

A	B	C	D	E
glanced	scowled	peered	snarled	raged

END OF TEST

YOU HAVE 16 QUESTIONS TO COMPLETE WITHIN THE TIME GIVEN.

Example i

Select the word that is most closely associated to the following word:

telephone

A	B	C	D	E
necklace	watch	bracelet	charm	ring

The correct answer is **E**. This has already been marked in Example i in Practice Test 9 of your answer sheet on page 155.

Example ii

Select the word that is most closely associated to the following word:

bunch

A	B	C	D	E
trees	keys	oranges	sweets	apples

The correct answer is **B**. Mark the answer B in Example ii in Practice Test 9 of your answer sheet on page 155.

For each row, select the word from the table that is most closely associated to the given word.

1 monarch

A	B	C	D	E
pencil	eraser	pen	ruler	compass

2 pride

A	B	C	D	E
tigers	bears	eagles	monkeys	lions

3 lucky

A	B	C	D	E
happy	day	try	wish	charm

4 table

A	B	C	D	E
add	list	graph	manners	drawers

5 celebrity

A	B	C	D	E
planet	moon	world	universe	star

6 book

A	B	C	D	E
amount	quantity	volume	area	ratio

7 eyes

A	B	C	D	E
whipped	peeled	stretched	squashed	rounded

8 lift

A	B	C	D	E
digger	drill	truck	crane	rope

Word Association

9 pen

A	B	C	D	E
sheep	horse	cow	cat	elephant

10 milk

A	B	C	D	E
whisk	churn	stir	beat	roll

11 tactile

A	B	C	D	E
fingers	ears	nose	mouth	hair

12 joke

A	B	C	D	E
ardour	vigour	candour	labour	humour

13 history

A	B	C	D	E
library	gallery	university	museum	zoo

14 oration

A	B	C	D	E
speech	hearing	smell	sight	touch

15 razor

A	B	C	D	E
pointed	fine	sharp	smooth	knife

16 coach

A	B	C	D	E
car	train	bike	ship	plane

END OF TEST

YOU HAVE 16 QUESTIONS TO COMPLETE WITHIN THE TIME GIVEN.

Example i

Four of these words are related in some way. Select the word that does not go with the other four.

A	B	C	D	E
plunge	fall	rise	drop	decrease

The correct answer is **C**. This has already been marked in Example i in Practice Test 10 of your answer sheet on page 155.

Example ii

Four of these words are related in some way. Select the word that does not go with the other four.

A	B	C	D	E
excited	interested	fascinated	intrigued	bored

The correct answer is **E**. Mark the answer E in Example ii in Practice Test 10 of your answer sheet on page 155.

In each set, four of the words are related in some way. Select the word that does not go with the other four.

1

A	B	C	D	E
football	swimming	cricket	hockey	tennis

2

A	B	C	D	E
cheese	eggs	milk	yoghurt	sugar

3

A	B	C	D	E
box	bowl	crate	chest	trunk

4

A	B	C	D	E
laugh	smile	frown	giggle	chuckle

5

A	B	C	D	E
rib	ankle	brain	hip	elbow

6

A	B	C	D	E
pea	carrot	potato	onion	turnip

7

A	B	C	D	E
peculiar	odd	strange	weird	usual

8

A	B	C	D	E
pig	sow	reap	plough	harvest

9

A	B	C	D	E
fair	honest	bright	sunny	fine

10

A	B	C	D	E
gaze	look	peer	view	scene

11

A	B	C	D	E
linen	wool	polyester	silk	cotton

12

A	B	C	D	E
follow	detect	track	trail	pursue

13

A	B	C	D	E
rain	shower	gale	drizzle	downpour

14

A	B	C	D	E
town	village	hamlet	city	cottage

15

A	B	C	D	E
swift	rapid	swallow	kestrel	osprey

16

A	B	C	D	E
climb	scale	ascend	reach	mount

END OF TEST

YOU HAVE 15 QUESTIONS TO COMPLETE WITHIN THE TIME GIVEN.

Example i

The following sentence is shuffled and also contains one unnecessary word. Rearrange the sentence correctly in order to identify the unnecessary word.

wake under before must sunrise up we.

A	B	C	D	E
up	before	under	wake	sunrise

The correct answer is **C**. This has already been marked in Example i in Practice Test 11 of your answer sheet on page 155.

Example ii

The following sentence is shuffled and also contains one unnecessary word. Rearrange the sentence correctly in order to identify the unnecessary word.

very girl quickly the ran throw.

A	B	C	D	E
quickly	girl	the	ran	throw

The correct answer is **E**. Mark the answer E in Example ii in Practice Test 11 of your answer sheet on page 155.

Each sentence below is shuffled and also contains one unnecessary word. Rearrange each sentence correctly in order to identify the unnecessary word.

1 boy eaten the the apple ate.

A	B	C	D	E
boy	the	apple	eaten	ate

2 years old Sarah eight was ate.

A	B	C	D	E
ate	was	years	eight	old

3 sped road flight car along the the.

A	B	C	D	E
road	car	flight	along	sped

4 animals crops the grew his farmer.

A	B	C	D	E
crops	animals	his	grew	farmer

5 lots we timing homework of had.

A	B	C	D	E
had	homework	we	timing	lots

6 desk lifted was made the of wood.

A	B	C	D	E
desk	lifted	of	wood	made

7 the most students enjoyed dislike of the course.

A	B	C	D	E
most	course	of	dislike	students

8 made to many mistakes too she.

A	B	C	D	E
made	to	she	mistakes	too

9 gaze the through wind forest the blew.

A	B	C	D	E
forest	blew	the	wind	gaze

10 and Noah family his open friends loved.

A	B	C	D	E
friends	family	and	open	loved

11 quickly boy the young into ran.

A	B	C	D	E
quickly	the	boy	young	into

12 capability inhabitants city's upset were the.

A	B	C	D	E
were	capability	the	inhabitants	upset

13 can prevent exercise illness figure help frequent.

A	B	C	D	E
prevent	illness	exercise	figure	frequent

14 the jury summarised lawyer four the case for the.

A	B	C	D	E
four	jury	case	summarised	lawyer

15 attacked suffer fellow his inmates prisoner the.

A	B	C	D	E
inmates	fellow	attacked	suffer	prisoner

END OF TEST

YOU HAVE 20 QUESTIONS TO COMPLETE WITHIN THE TIME GIVEN.

Example i

Read the sentence below and select the most appropriate word from the table.

A	B	C	D	E
defeated	heaved	master	flow	politely

The skilful chess player easily **Question ①** his opponent.

Select your answer to go in the place of **Question ①** in the above sentence.

The correct answer is **A**. This has already been marked in Example i in Practice Test 12 of your answer sheet on page 155.

Example ii

Read the sentence below and select the most appropriate word from the table.

A	B	C	D	E
crunching	eating	dreading	reading	shining

The sun was **Question ②** and there was not a single cloud in the sky.

Select your answer to go in the place of **Question ②** in the above sentence.

The correct answer is **E**. Mark the answer E in Example ii in Practice Test 12 of your answer sheet on page 155.

Read the passage and select the most appropriate word from the table below by choosing the letter above the word. There are 10 questions.

A	B	C	D	E
minutes	found	strong	adequate	absorbed

F	G	H	I	J
essential	deficiency	pills	directly	brittle

Vitamin D

Vitamin D is Question ① for maintaining healthy and Question ② teeth and bones. Luckily, Vitamin D can be Question ③ by the body Question ④ from sunlight.

On a clear summer's day, Question ⑤ amounts of Vitamin D can be produced by the body if you spend just ten Question ⑥ per day outside. However, in winter, this process can require up to two hours. Therefore, many people suffer from a Vitamin D Question ⑦ in winter. This can cause their bones to become Question ⑧ and can also trigger mental illnesses such as depression.

Fortunately, Vitamin D can also be Question ⑨ naturally in certain foods such as butter and eggs. Some people also take Question ⑩ and supplements to boost their Vitamin D levels.

Read the passage and select the most appropriate word from the table below by choosing the letter above the word. There are 10 questions.

A	B	C	D	E
estimate	death	fought	crowned	morning

F	G	H	I	J
flee	forces	significant	army	attempts

The Battle of Hastings

The Battle of Hastings was **Question 11** in 1066 between the Norman **Question 12** of William the

Conqueror and an English army led by King Harold Godwinson.

Historians **Question 13** that 15,000 soldiers took part in the battle. The two **Question 14** attacked

each other from **Question 15** until evening. Finally, Harold was struck and killed by an arrow and the

English began to **Question 16** .

William was **Question 17** king later that year and ruled over England until his **Question 18** in

1087. The Battle of Hastings was a **Question 19** turning point in English history. Despite many

Question 20 , no foreign army ever successfully managed to invade England after 1066.

END OF TEST

THIS PAGE HAS DELIBERATELY BEEN LEFT BLANK

Collins

11+
Verbal Reasoning

Assessment

Workbook

THIS PAGE HAS DELIBERATELY BEEN LEFT BLANK

Collins

Verbal Reasoning Assessment Paper 1

Instructions:

1. Ensure you have pencils and an eraser with you.
2. Make sure you are able to see a clock or watch.
3. Write your name on the answer sheet.
4. Do not open the question booklet until you are told to do so by an adult.
5. Mark your answers on the answer sheet only.
6. All workings must be completed on a separate piece of paper.
7. You should not use a calculator, dictionary or thesaurus at any point in this paper.
8. Move through the sections as quickly as possible and with care.
9. Follow the instructions at the foot of each page.
10. You should mark your answers with a horizontal strike, as shown on the answer sheet.
11. If you want to change your answer, ensure that you rub out your first answer and that your second answer is clearly more visible.
12. You can go back and review any questions that are within the section you are working on only.

You should await further instructions before moving onto another section.

Symbols and Phrases used in the Tests

 Instructions

 Time allowed for this section

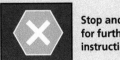 Stop and wait for further instructions

 Continue working

THIS PAGE HAS DELIBERATELY BEEN LEFT BLANK

SECTION 1: COMPREHENSION

We didn't realise what had happened until we heard a helicopter passing over the roof of our house. It was an air ambulance and it landed next to the main road. One of our neighbours then told us that there had been a car crash near the corner shop and somebody was seriously injured.

Example i

What landed next to the main road?

A   A plane

B   A hot-air balloon

C   A glider

D   A helicopter

The correct answer is **D**. This has already been marked in Example i in Section 1 of your answer sheet on page 157.

Example ii

Who said there had been a car accident?

A   A neighbour

B   A police officer

C   A paramedic

D   A shopkeeper

The correct answer is **A**. Mark the answer A in Example ii in Section 1 of your answer sheet on page 157.

Carefully read through the following passage and answer the questions that follow.

Mark your answer on the answer sheet by choosing from the options A–D.

Bleak House

by Charles Dickens

Richard, Ada, and Esther (the narrator) are in London. They accompany an old lady to her house and, on the way, meet Mr Krook who runs a shop and is obsessed with the nearby law courts.

She had stopped at a shop over which was written KROOK, RAG AND BOTTLE WAREHOUSE. Also, in long thin letters, KROOK, DEALER IN MARINE STORES. In one part of the window was a picture of a red paper mill at which a cart was unloading a quantity of sacks of old rags. In another was the inscription BONES BOUGHT. In another, KITCHEN-STUFF BOUGHT. In another, OLD IRON BOUGHT. In another, WASTE-PAPER BOUGHT. In another, LADIES' AND GENTLEMEN'S WARDROBES BOUGHT. Everything seemed to be bought and nothing to be sold there. In all parts of the window were quantities of dirty bottles—blacking bottles, medicine bottles, ginger-beer and soda-water bottles, pickle bottles, wine bottles, ink bottles; I am reminded by mentioning the latter that the shop had in several little particulars the air of being in a legal neighbourhood and of being, as it were, a dirty hanger-on and disowned relation of the law. There were a great many ink bottles. There was a little tottering bench of shabby old volumes outside the door, labelled "Law Books, all at 9d." [...] There were several second-hand bags, blue and red, hanging up. A little way within the shop-door lay heaps of old crackled parchment scrolls and discoloured and dog's-eared law-papers. I could have fancied that all the rusty keys, of which there must have been hundreds huddled together as old iron, had once belonged to doors of rooms or strong chests in lawyers' offices. The litter of rags tumbled partly into and partly out of a one-legged wooden scale, hanging without any counterpoise from a beam, might have been counsellors' bands and gowns torn up. One had only to fancy, as Richard whispered to Ada and me while we all stood looking in, that yonder bones in a corner, piled together and picked very clean, were the bones of clients, to make the picture complete.

As it was still foggy and dark, and as the shop was blinded besides by the wall of Lincoln's Inn, intercepting the light within a couple of yards, we should not have seen so much but for a lighted lantern that an old man in spectacles and a hairy cap was carrying about in the shop. Turning towards the door, he now caught sight of us. He was short, cadaverous, and withered, with his head sunk sideways between his shoulders and the breath issuing in visible smoke from his mouth as if he were on fire within. His throat, chin, and eyebrows were so frosted with white hairs and so gnarled with veins and puckered skin that he looked from his breast upward like some old root in a fall of snow.

CONTINUE WORKING

"Hi, hi!" said the old man, coming to the door. "Have you anything to sell?"

[…]

"My landlord, Krook," said the little old lady, condescending to him from her lofty station as she presented him to us. "He is called among the neighbours the Lord Chancellor. His shop is called the Court of Chancery. He is a very eccentric person. He is very odd. Oh, I assure you he is very odd!"

She shook her head a great many times and tapped her forehead with her finger to express to us that we must have the goodness to excuse him, "For he is a little—you know—M!" said the old lady with great stateliness. The old man overheard, and laughed.

"It's true enough," he said, going before us with the lantern, "that they call me the Lord Chancellor and call my shop Chancery. And why do you think they call me the Lord Chancellor and my shop Chancery?"

"I don't know, I am sure!" said Richard rather carelessly.

"You see," said the old man, stopping and turning round, "they—Hi! Here's lovely hair! I have got three sacks of ladies' hair below, but none so beautiful and fine as this. What colour, and what texture!"

"That'll do, my good friend!" said Richard, strongly disapproving of his having drawn one of Ada's tresses through his yellow hand. "You can admire as the rest of us do without taking that liberty."

The old man darted at him a sudden look which even called my attention from Ada, who, startled and blushing, was so remarkably beautiful that she seemed to fix the wandering attention of the little old lady herself. But as Ada interposed and laughingly said she could only feel proud of such genuine admiration, Mr. Krook shrunk into his former self as suddenly as he had leaped out of it.

---

1 **According to paragraph 1, what is the shop window full of?**

A Old books about law

B Pictures

C Signs and bottles

D Sacks full of rags and parchments

CONTINUE WORKING

2 What does the narrator notice about the shop?

A It has a lot of strange things for sale.

B It offers to buy things rather than sell them.

C It is pleasantly decorated.

D It doesn't contain much stock.

3 What colour bags are on sale?

A Blue and green

B Green and red

C Red and yellow

D Blue and red

4 What does the narrator mean when she describes the shop as being like 'a dirty hanger-on and disowned relation'?

A The shop looks unclean and unwanted.

B The shop is too full of different goods.

C The shop is full of people who look unclean.

D The shop is full of filthy clothes hung from the ceiling.

5 Which of these is not said to be bought or sold by Mr Krook?

A Waste paper

B Wine

C Bones

D Clothes

6 What does the narrator notice about the keys?

A They are many of them piled up in a large chest.

B They are wrapped in old rags.

C They are rusty and hanging from Krook's belt.

D There are lots of them and they are rusty.

CONTINUE WORKING

7 What does it mean when the law papers are described as 'discoloured and dog's-eared'.

   A The papers are old and no one wants them.

   B The papers have been screwed up and left.

   C The papers look old and are folded at the corners.

   D The papers have had something spilled on them.

8 Why does Richard whisper to Ada and the narrator at the end of paragraph 1?

   A He's making an impolite joke and doesn't want Mr Krook to hear.

   B He's sharing a secret with the two girls and doesn't want to be overheard.

   C He doesn't want to admit out loud that he finds the shop sinister.

   D He is worried that Mr Krook may have killed one of the previous customers.

9 At the start of paragraph 2, the narrator describes a wall 'intercepting the light within a couple of yards' of Mr Krook's shop.

   What does this mean?

   A The wall is built too close to the shop.

   B The front wall of the shop is in direct sunlight.

   C The wall stops any light escaping from the shop.

   D The wall stops much light from reaching the shop.

10 The narrator compares Mr Krook to 'some old root in a fall of snow'.

   What reason is given for this?

   A He is old and shivering.

   B His face is withered and covered in white hairs.

   C He is very thin and surrounded by scraps of rags.

   D His skin is very pale and wrinkly.

11 What is Mr Krook carrying when the narrator first sees him?

   A His spectacles

   B A cat

   C A lantern

   D Some keys

CONTINUE WORKING

12 What does the author mean when Mr Krook is described as 'eccentric'?

A His behaviour is unusual and strange.

B His behaviour is rude and aggressive.

C His behaviour is funny and surprising.

D His behaviour is sinister and discomforting.

13 '"My landlord, Krook," said the little old lady, condescending to him from her lofty station as she presented him to us.'

What does the word 'presented' mean in this context?

A Introduced

B Gave

C Delivered

D Exhibited

14 How does the old lady behave when talking about Mr Krook?

A As if she is mad

B As if she is important

C As if she doesn't know much about him

D As if she is frightened of him

15 Which word best describes Mr Krook's nickname of the 'Lord Chancellor'?

A Cruelty

B Irony

C Hyperbole

D Simile

16 Richard's speech is described using the adverb 'carelessly'.

What is an adverb?

A A word that describes a noun.

B A word ending in -ly.

C A word that describes an adjective.

D A word that describes a verb.

CONTINUE WORKING

17 What does Mr Krook like about Ada's hair?

   A How it looks and feels

   B Its colour and length

   C The style in which it has been cut

   D Its texture and cleanliness

18 Which of the following doesn't the old lady do when talking about Mr Krook?

   A Shake her head

   B Tap her head with her finger

   C Leave her sentence unfinished

   D Take hold of Krook's lantern

19 What does Mr Krook keep downstairs in his shop?

   A A display of wigs

   B Bags of women's hair

   C Fine material

   D The bones of previous customers

20 How does Richard behave towards Ada?

   A Loving

   B Careless

   C Protective

   D Angry

21 What does Richard suggest Krook do when he becomes interested in Ada's hair?

   A Buy it.

   B Look but not touch.

   C Stroke it more gently.

   D Wash his hands.

CONTINUE WORKING

22 What does the author mean when writing, 'The old man darted at him a sudden look'?

   A Krook moves suddenly towards Richard.

   B Krook throws something at Richard.

   C Krook becomes interested in Richard's hair.

   D Krook looks quickly at Richard.

23 How does Ada respond to Mr Krook's behaviour?

   A She is surprised and embarrassed.

   B She is shocked and revolted.

   C She is nervous and disgusted.

   D She is grateful and happy.

24 What does the author mean when writing that Ada 'interposed'?

   A She draws attention to herself because she doesn't like being ignored.

   B She asks a question about why Krook liked her hair so much.

   C She interrupts to stop any conflict between Richard and Mr Krook.

   D She stands between the two men to get their attention.

25 What does the author suggest about Mr Krook when describing how he, 'shrunk into his former self as suddenly as he had leaped out of it'?

   A His behaviour is unpredictable.

   B He moves very quickly.

   C He's very shy.

   D He isn't the man he once was.

STOP AND WAIT FOR FURTHER INSTRUCTIONS

SECTION 2: SYNONYMS

Example i

Select the word that is most similar in meaning to the following word:

cold

A	B	C	D	E
wet	fence	foggy	windy	chilly

The correct answer is **E**. This has already been marked in Example i in Section 2 of your answer sheet on page 157.

Example ii

Select the word that is most similar in meaning to the following word:

start

A	B	C	D	E
cramped	begin	free	without	change

The correct answer is **B**. Mark the answer B in Example ii in Section 2 of your answer sheet on page 157.

STOP AND WAIT FOR FURTHER INSTRUCTIONS

In each question, select the word from the table that is most similar in meaning to the word above the table.

1 brief

A	B	C	D	E
accuracy	exclamation	confidence	case	instruction

2 shepherd

A	B	C	D	E
prepare	chaperone	distinguish	imprison	sheep

3 vessel

A	B	C	D	E
garment	clock	container	sundial	mast

4 divert

A	B	C	D	E
imply	differ	exchange	deflect	disable

5 notion

A	B	C	D	E
emergency	system	indication	distinction	idea

6 persistent

A	B	C	D	E
determined	half-hearted	unsure	desperation	contained

7 opaque

A	B	C	D	E
dense	transparent	bright	translucent	glacial

8 dubious

A	B	C	D	E
thrilled	fantastic	sceptical	annoying	double

CONTINUE WORKING

9 pessimism

A	B	C	D	E
positivity	fulfilment	insolence	degrade	negativity

10 succumb

A	B	C	D	E
determine	tempt	decline	surrender	suppose

11 vacant

A	B	C	D	E
unoccupied	locked	close	congested	unavailable

12 restrained

A	B	C	D	E
distraught	wild	unhindered	fallible	controlled

13 dispersal

A	B	C	D	E
strewn	spread	vanish	disappearance	unforgiving

14 illicit

A	B	C	D	E
illiterate	unpleasant	indicative	unlawful	inevitable

15 whimsical

A	B	C	D	E
playful	boring	calm	furious	blatant

16 shimmer

A	B	C	D	E
flow	shiver	shake	explode	glisten

CONTINUE WORKING

17 innocuous

A	B	C	D	E
guilty	indecisive	unbearable	harmless	harmful

18 partisan

A	B	C	D	E
leader	host	supporter	guard	prisoner

19 insinuate

A	B	C	D	E
insist	instigate	imply	deduce	declaration

20 abuse

A	B	C	D	E
exploit	nurture	distinguish	care	behaviour

21 fundamental

A	B	C	D	E
important	unbalanced	basic	tragic	superior

22 congregation

A	B	C	D	E
parliament	government	gathering	exception	mixture

23 flawed

A	B	C	D	E
frail	faulty	failure	disgraced	embarrassed

24 impediment

A	B	C	D	E
implement	caution	implication	inability	hindrance

STOP AND WAIT FOR FURTHER INSTRUCTIONS

SECTION 3: DEFINITIONS

 INSTRUCTIONS

 YOU HAVE 6 MINUTES TO COMPLETE THE FOLLOWING SECTION.

YOU HAVE 24 QUESTIONS TO COMPLETE WITHIN THE TIME GIVEN.

Example i

The teacher said the standard of conduct in the class was distinctly average.

What does the word 'conduct' mean?

A	B	C	D	E
music	learning	teaching	behaviour	smartness

The correct answer is **D**. This has already been marked in Example i in Section 3 of your answer sheet on page 158.

Example ii

In summer it is nice to go out at dusk when all is tranquil.

What does the word 'tranquil' mean?

A	B	C	D	E
silent	warm	peaceful	dark	pleasant

The correct answer is **C**. Mark the answer C in Example ii in Section 3 of your answer sheet on page 158.

STOP AND WAIT FOR FURTHER INSTRUCTIONS

Read each sentence and select the most appropriate word to answer the questions.

To make a cake, first ensure that you have sufficient ingredients and the necessary equipment.

1 What does the word 'sufficient' mean?

A	B	C	D	E
sweet	various	spare	enough	inadequate

2 What does the word 'necessary' mean?

A	B	C	D	E
total	essential	finest	most	biggest

At the consultation, the doctor said he would prescribe a new medication for me.

3 What does the word 'prescribe' mean?

A	B	C	D	E
write	invent	ban	order	reserve

4 What is 'medication'?

A	B	C	D	E
cure	medicine	bandage	appointment	symptom

The solicitor said her client had shown complete remorse for his crimes.

5 What does the word 'solicitor' mean?

A	B	C	D	E
witness	court	jury	judge	lawyer

6 What does the word 'remorse' mean?

A	B	C	D	E
sadness	sorrow	regret	pity	sympathy

The weather in the mountains was dismal so the rescue mission had to be postponed.

7 What does the word 'dismal' mean?

A	B	C	D	E
cloudy	boring	grey	miserable	dangerous

8 What does the word 'postponed' mean?

A	B	C	D	E
accelerated	cancelled	delayed	completed	started

CONTINUE WORKING

The newly built bridge is a highly acclaimed feat of engineering.

9 What does the word 'acclaimed' mean?

A	B	C	D	E
praised	publicised	complicated	expensive	useful

10 What is a 'feat'?

A	B	C	D	E
structure	piece	accomplishment	type	project

The champions processed through the town on an open-top bus before receiving the cheers of the multitude in the main square.

11 What does the word 'processed' mean'?

A	B	C	D	E
marched	danced	paraded	celebrated	rode

12 What is a 'multitude'?

A	B	C	D	E
group	spectator	mob	crowd	army

Some glaciers have seen ice become detached and others have gradually contracted.

13 What does the word 'detached' mean?

A	B	C	D	E
joined	melted	hardened	merged	separated

14 What does the word 'contract' mean?

A	B	C	D	E
agree	shrink	expand	sink	break

The camera crew trekked through the jungle for three days before spotting the monkeys high in the tree canopy.

15 What does the word 'trek' mean?

A	B	C	D	E
track	drive	ramble	hike	hack

16 What is a 'canopy'?

A	B	C	D	E
cover	cage	branch	forest	skyline

CONTINUE WORKING

It is often said that laughter is a potent remedy when someone is feeling under the weather.

17 What does the word 'potent' mean?

A	B	C	D	E
possible	useful	simple	powerful	magical

18 What is a 'remedy'?

A	B	C	D	E
aid	cure	effect	boost	benefit

One factor in global warming is the discharge of greenhouse gases.

19 What does the word 'factor' mean?

A	B	C	D	E
problem	reason	fraction	element	explanation

20 What is a 'discharge'?

A	B	C	D	E
volume	release	measurement	type	level

The soprano was renowned for being able to sustain higher notes longer than anyone else.

21 What does the word 'renowned' mean?

A	B	C	D	E
applauded	noted	infamous	popular	unknown

22 What does the word 'sustain' mean?

A	B	C	D	E
sing	try	reach	hold	produce

The scientist's achievements in his chosen field are unsurpassed and he deserves this accolade.

23 What does the word 'unsurpassed' mean?

A	B	C	D	E
unrivalled	untested	undoubted	unbeatable	brilliant

24 What is an 'accolade'?

A	B	C	D	E
glory	fame	recognition	celebration	career

STOP AND WAIT FOR FURTHER INSTRUCTIONS

SECTION 4: SHUFFLED SENTENCES

INSTRUCTIONS

 YOU HAVE 11 MINUTES TO COMPLETE THE FOLLOWING SECTION.

YOU HAVE 22 QUESTIONS TO COMPLETE WITHIN THE TIME GIVEN.

Example i

The following sentence is shuffled and also contains one unnecessary word. Rearrange the sentence correctly in order to identify the unnecessary word.

dog the ran fetch the to stick eating.

A	B	C	D	E
eating	dog	ran	the	stick

The correct answer is **A**. This has already been marked in Example i in Section 4 of your answer sheet on page 158.

Example ii

The following sentence is shuffled and also contains one unnecessary word. Rearrange the sentence correctly in order to identify the unnecessary word.

pushed Emma stood up and closed the table under the chairs.

A	B	C	D	E
chairs	stood	under	closed	Emma

The correct answer is **D**. Mark the answer D in Example ii in Section 4 of your answer sheet on page 158.

STOP AND WAIT FOR FURTHER INSTRUCTIONS

Each sentence below is shuffled and also contains one unnecessary word. Rearrange each sentence correctly in order to identify the unnecessary word.

1   her Mum been telling indication in Kerala childhood about us has.

A	B	C	D	E
childhood	telling	indication	about	Kerala

2   took the dog along the picture towpath her morning they for walk.

A	B	C	D	E
picture	along	towpath	walk	the

3   today unbelievably the traffic has lights been heavy inner city.

A	B	C	D	E
lights	traffic	today	inner	been

4   finally Freya to the flour and egg added butter flower mixture.

A	B	C	D	E
the	flour	flower	and	mixture

5   apart it children went outside was heavily although the raining.

A	B	C	D	E
although	went	raining	apart	it

6   vase and put the petals with water roses in a glass filled it Ali.

A	B	C	D	E
with	put	it	roses	petals

7   how the effecting nature programme affecting showed warming global is the Arctic.

A	B	C	D	E
affecting	how	the	effecting	nature

CONTINUE WORKING

8 we had so coats and it was cold to put on our hot hats.

A	B	C	D	E
hot	we	hats	put	so

9 but his teacher's upset tried to attention get times without he many success.

A	B	C	D	E
tried	success	upset	without	attention

10 we decided neighbours were quite upset abroad to when our garage move.

A	B	C	D	E
our	garage	to	quite	move

11 the boat moored the captain plane the quayside at.

A	B	C	D	E
boat	moored	captain	the	plane

12 the wait shelf under the collapsed so many books of weight.

A	B	C	D	E
many	wait	under	weight	so

13 invited me want to at his party Jake has but to I don't go.

A	B	C	D	E
want	has	at	to	his

14 from Maire two couldn't wait her cousins last to see Australia.

A	B	C	D	E
last	Maire	cousins	to	her

15 the easy runners gruelling exhausted were after the race.

A	B	C	D	E
the	after	were	easy	race

CONTINUE WORKING

16 Val's able to desperate computer means she is much faster new work.

A	B	C	D	E
to	much	desperate	new	able

17 are blocked we need our cleaner for a professional chimney.

A	B	C	D	E
our	chimney	for	are	need

18 it's plenty of important and have to people diet a balanced exercise.

A	B	C	D	E
plenty	people	balanced	it's	have

19 Henry VIII we the life of discussed after queen the documentary watching.

A	B	C	D	E
we	the	of	after	queen

20 with barely to spare they a minute boarded captain the plane.

A	B	C	D	E
captain	boarded	they	to	spare

21 the builders complete a long time pushing are the extension to taking.

A	B	C	D	E
the	time	pushing	taking	are

22 the amount of our school holiday fair an amazing money for raised new playground.

A	B	C	D	E
amazing	new	our	money	holiday

STOP AND WAIT FOR FURTHER INSTRUCTIONS

SECTION 5: CLOZE

 YOU HAVE 12 MINUTES TO COMPLETE THE FOLLOWING SECTION.

YOU HAVE 28 QUESTIONS TO COMPLETE WITHIN THE TIME GIVEN.

Example i

Read the sentence below and select the most appropriate word from the table.

A	B	C	D	E
backdrop	carefully	drawer	disadvantage	dilution

The undulating hills were the perfect **Question 1** for the watercolour painting.

Select your answer to go in the place of **Question 1** in the above sentence. The correct answer is **A**. This has already been marked in Example i in Section 5 of your answer sheet on page 158.

Example ii

Read the sentence below and select the most appropriate word from the table.

A	B	C	D	E
had	interior	success	attend	absent

The girl decided she would like to **Question 2** the party.

Select your answer to go in the place of **Question 2** in the above sentence. The correct answer is **D**. Mark the answer D in Example ii in Section 5 of your answer sheet on page 158.

STOP AND WAIT FOR FURTHER INSTRUCTIONS

Read the passage and select the most appropriate words from the table below, using each once.

A	B	C	D	E
sets	soldiers	Crete	view	labyrinth

F	G	H	I	J
prison	death	conquer	stone	soared

Daedalus and Icarus

Hearing that Daedalus had helped Theseus to **Question 1** the Minotaur in the **Question 2**, King Minos of Crete was furious and cast Daedalus and his son Icarus into **Question 3**. Although Daedalus felt sure he could escape, he knew it would be impossible to leave the island of Crete by sea as the king's **Question 4** would be watching the ships.

Using his expertise as a craftsman, Daedalus made two **Question 5** of feathered wings, fastening them with thread and wax. Instructing his son to fly neither too high nor too low, the two men beat their wings and flew away from **Question 6**. Icarus grew bolder and **Question 7** up and up, shouting in delight at the **Question 8** below. Closer and closer to the Sun he flew, whereupon the wax which held his feathers together melted and he dropped like a **Question 9** out of the sky, plunging to his **Question 10** into the waters below.

CONTINUE WORKING

Read the passage and select the most appropriate words from the table below, using each once.

A	B	C	D	E
wildlife	issue	congestion	granted	travesty

F	G	H	I	J
heritage	object	response	accept	think

Response from Major Dodds

Dear Councillor McPherson,

I am writing to **Question 11** to the planning permission that has been **Question 12** for a leisure centre in the woodland area on the outskirts of our town.

I'm shocked that such a notion has even passed the preliminary planning stages! This is such a beautiful and precious part of our historic town's **Question 13** and would be sorely missed by every member of the community. Can you really justify such a **Question 14**?

Not only would we miss our woodland walks and picnics, **Question 15** would also be a casualty. Where do you think the badgers, frogs, birds and insects will go when bulldozers and diggers start piling in? We are so lucky to have this area of natural beauty, lush with all sorts of wild flowers and shrubs. I go there with my art class most weekends to sketch, paint and take photographs.

A further concern is traffic **Question 16** – as you well know, Brumborough is a mere 3 miles away and its inhabitants will be desperate to come to use the leisure facilities. Traffic is already an **Question 17** but this would only compound it further. As for car parking – don't get me started on that!

I hope you will take my concerns about this issue seriously. I fully **Question 18** that there will be many people who want this leisure facility to go ahead but I can **Question 19** of other towns where there would be less of a negative impact.

I look forward to hearing your **Question 20** as soon as possible.

Yours sincerely,

Major Clifford Dodds

CONTINUE WORKING

In these passages, some of the words are missing. Complete the passages by selecting the best set of words for each question. Mark your answer on the answer sheet by choosing one of the options A–E. Each set of words can only be used once.

Questions 21–24

The descent to the castle dungeon was by a winding staircase. Forty steps Question **21** behind which was a single cell. The cell had stone walls from which a pair of manacles and chains hung. There was no sign of a window so that Question **22** the prisoner was cut off from all sight and sound from the outside world. Summer or winter, night or day, rain or shine Question **23** However, at one end of the cell stood an oaken table Question **24** So there could be an escape of sorts after all – via a writer's imagination!

A	on which were writing materials including a quill.
B	were all the same down here.
C	led to a huge, thick metal door
D	the dungeon consisted of a row of cells
E	when the door clanged shut

Questions 25–28

It seemed rather incongruous to say the least to find one of the cathedral apses Question **25** about the size of a two-person dome tent. It was largely silvery grey in colour but some parts of its surface were blackened with what looked like scorch marks. It was, in fact, the Soyuz space capsule which had brought three astronauts safely back to earth Question **26** and was now being displayed in various locations around the country. The scorch marks, it turned out, were caused by the heat created Question **27** This was the most hazardous part of the whole trip as the capsule had to enter the atmosphere at just the right angle Question **28**

A	occupied by a cone-shaped, metallic object
B	as the capsule re-entered the earth's atmosphere.
C	or it could have completely burned up.
D	carried out lots of scientific experiments
E	after six months spent on the International Space Station

END OF PAPER

Collins

Verbal Reasoning Assessment Paper 2

Instructions:

1. Ensure you have pencils and an eraser with you.
2. Make sure you are able to see a clock or watch.
3. Write your name on the answer sheet.
4. Do not open the question booklet until you are told to do so by an adult.
5. Mark your answers on the answer sheet only.
6. All workings must be completed on a separate piece of paper.
7. You should not use a calculator, dictionary or thesaurus at any point in this paper.
8. Move through the sections as quickly as possible and with care.
9. Follow the instructions at the foot of each page.
10. You should mark your answers with a horizontal strike, as shown on the answer sheet.
11. If you want to change your answer, ensure that you rub out your first answer and that your second answer is clearly more visible.
12. You can go back and review any questions that are within the section you are working on only.

You should await further instructions before moving onto another section.

Symbols and Phrases used in the Tests

 Instructions
 Time allowed for this section
 Stop and wait for further instructions
 Continue working

THIS PAGE HAS DELIBERATELY BEEN LEFT BLANK

SECTION 1: COMPREHENSION

 INSTRUCTIONS

 YOU HAVE 15 MINUTES TO COMPLETE THE FOLLOWING SECTION.

YOU HAVE 25 QUESTIONS TO COMPLETE WITHIN THE TIME GIVEN.

We didn't realise what had happened until we heard a helicopter passing over the roof of our house. It was an air ambulance and it landed next to the main road. One of our neighbours then told us that there had been a car crash near the corner shop and somebody was seriously injured.

Example i

What landed next to the main road?

A A plane

B A hot-air balloon

C A glider

D A helicopter

The correct answer is **D**. This has already been marked in Example i in Section 1 of your answer sheet on page 159.

Example ii

Who said there had been a car accident?

A A neighbour

B A police officer

C A paramedic

D A shopkeeper

The correct answer is **A**. Mark the answer A in Example ii in Section 1 of your answer sheet on page 159.

STOP AND WAIT FOR FURTHER INSTRUCTIONS

Carefully read through the following passage and answer the questions that follow.

Mark your answer on the answer sheet by choosing from the options A–D.

Mount Yasur: To Hell and Back

by James Draven

"I know it looks terrifying, but most of what you can see is just clouds of gas and ash…" says a British geologist, casually addressing his holiday companions as they hug their knees at his feet. They can see nothing of course, with their eyes screwed up tight in the darkness and their backs turned to Hades, but a great, noxious blaze of biblical brimstone seethes with nebulous incandescence above our heads.

John, my new geologist acquaintance, and I are standing on the very brink of a precipice of crumbling black rock; beneath us churns a literal lake of fire. I peer down into the pit and at that moment the air reverberates with an omnipresent roar, and a searing, sulphurous wind blasts my face, toasting my brow, momentarily blinding me, and sweeping me off my feet. A jet of 1,000°C liquid rock shoots heavenward.

Now I'm kneeling with the rest of the congregation and, in the absence of health and safety legislation, using the crater's rim both as a handrail to stop myself tumbling backward into inky oblivion to meet my maker, and as a shield from the wrath of hellfire before me. Meanwhile, John — still just about standing — continues his laid-back lecture on lava: spouting rock-solid facts to reassure his petrified friends.

"… And the magma is illuminating that ash cloud, which makes it look much worse than it actually is…" he says, like a mollycoddling date at a horror movie, throwing a metaphorical arm around quivering shoulders and explaining that it's not real; it's all smoke and mirrors. As I regain my feet, a very animated — but definitely non-CGI — animal flaps across the face of the yawning abyss, its outstretched leathery wings silhouetted against the churning inferno below: a bat out of Hell.

Mount Yasur is touted as the world's most accessible active volcano because, with the right vehicle, you can drive to within 200 metres of its vents, which have been erupting nearly continuously for over 800 years. Located on the remote island of Tanna in the South Pacific archipelago of Vanuatu, the entrance is a two-hour trip from the airport, first through lush forests and then across a barren ash plane of shifting, gunmetal grains of sand, and brittle threads of 'Pele's hair': airborne molten lava caught by the wind and spun out into delicate strands, named after the Hawaiian fire goddess.

Only a few months ago, a cyclone tore across this countryside but, rising phoenix-like from the ashes of destruction, the locals have rebuilt and replanted. The only traces of this act of God are the sheets of

CONTINUE WORKING

corrugated iron that remain twisted like sweet wrappers in lofty tree branches along the arduous, pitted track towards the volcano: a route I've named the Road to Hell.

In truth, the underworld we now gaze upon is far from purgatory. Peering into this mesmeric magma chamber is like staring into the eye of the Creator, and up here on this diabolical mountaintop, geologist John's sermon on stone means nothing more than the ravings of a crazed street preacher. He may be a scientist, a scholar, and an expert on the phenomenon we're witnessing, but watching as Mother Earth gives fiery birth defies rational explanation.

As pandemonium finally subsides, John's friends beat a hasty retreat back around the rim's circumference and down to the base, leaving us alone with our awe. I ask him how many volcanoes he's visited, and he surprises me with his answer:

"This is my first," he says.

My eyebrows shoot upwards, and he qualifies his answer with a devilish gleam in his eyes:

"Having studied these things in great detail, I've never thought standing on the edge of an active volcano is a terribly sensible place to be."

1 **In paragraph 1, how is the geologist presented as being different to his holiday companions?**

   A He is much older than they are.

   B He is calm whereas they are frightened.

   C He is British but they are not.

   D He is looking upwards while they are looking down into the volcano.

2 **Why does the phrase, 'very brink of a precipice', make what they are doing sound dangerous?**

   A It shows they are about to fall into the volcano.

   B It shows that rocks are likely to fall onto them.

   C It shows they are squeezed into a very tight space.

   D It shows they are at the edge of the volcano.

3 **Which of these is not an effect that the 'sulphurous wind' has on the writer in paragraph 2?**

   A He is disgusted by the smell of sulphur.

   B His face feels very hot.

   C He cannot see.

   D He is knocked over.

CONTINUE WORKING

4 What does the writer mean by an 'omnipresent roar' in paragraph 2?

 A The roar of the volcano is very loud.

 B There is a constant roaring noise all around them.

 C The roar of the volcano is the only thing they can hear.

 D The volcano seems very powerful.

5 According to paragraph 2, what is the writer's relationship with John, the geologist?

 A He knows him a little but they've only recently met.

 B Although they've only just met, they have become very close friends.

 C He doesn't trust him as he has taken them so close to the volcano.

 D They've known each other for a while and get along okay.

6 In paragraph 3, what does the writer do to try to make himself feel safer?

 A He kneels down.

 B He grips the edge of the crater.

 C He listens to John's lecture.

 D He begins to pray.

7 What do the words 'seethes' (paragraph 1) and 'wrath' (paragraph 3) suggest about the volcano?

 A The volcano is angry with the tourists.

 B It is a very large and beautiful volcano.

 C It is a dangerously active volcano.

 D The volcano is seconds from eruption.

8 According to John in paragraph 4, why don't they need to be afraid?

 A They can watch from a vehicle if they prefer to.

 B There's plenty of light so they're not in danger.

 C Because if he can keep on his feet so can they.

 D The ash cloud isn't actually on fire, it's just being lit up by the volcano.

CONTINUE WORKING

9 What does the writer mean by the phrase, 'throwing a metaphorical arm around quivering shoulders', in paragraph 4?

   A John is going around reassuring each person but he can't do it to everyone.

   B John is pretending that everything's safe to make them all feel better.

   C It feels like John is comforting them but he's doing it with his words rather than physically.

   D Everyone is scared except John so he puts his arms around them.

10 Mount Yasur is described as the world's most accessible active volcano.

   What reason is given for this in paragraph 5?

   A You can walk quickly from the nearest airport to the volcano.

   B If you have suitable transport, you don't have to walk far to reach the volcano.

   C You can drive a car up to the very rim of the volcano.

   D There is a clear route leading up the last 200 metres of the volcano.

11 In paragraph 4, what does the writer mean when he links the volcano to 'smoke and mirrors'?

   A The ash cloud is making them scared and they can see their fear on each other's faces.

   B Despite the smoke, they can see their reflections in the volcano's lava.

   C The volcano is like a big magic trick and isn't really there.

   D Their fear is based on an illusion because the volcano isn't as dangerous as it looks.

12 What do we find out from paragraph 5 about the island of Tanna?

   A The island is part of the Vanuatu archipelago in the Pacific Ocean.

   B The island is remote and can be found in the Pacific archipelago.

   C The island is in the Pacific Ocean but is so remote that it's almost impossible to get to.

   D The island is also called Vanuatu and is near the Pacific Ocean.

13 Paragraph 5 says, 'the entrance is a two-hour trip from the airport, first through lush forests and then across a barren ash plane'.

   What is the meaning of 'plane' in this context?

   A A colourless area

   B A perfectly level surface

   C An aeroplane

   D A flat landscape

CONTINUE WORKING

14 In paragraph 5, what is 'Pele's hair'?

   A A Hawaiian fire goddess

   B Thin strands of lava that have cooled and hardened in the wind

   C Grains of sand mixed with molten lava

   D Drops of molten lava that are drifting through the air

15 In paragraph 5, what evidence is given to show that the volcano is active?

   A There have been several eruptions over the last 800 years.

   B There have been frequent eruptions over the last 800 years.

   C There have been a few eruptions over the last 800 years.

   D There have been 800 eruptions in the last year.

16 Which statement best describes the effect of the simile, 'sheets of corrugated iron that remain twisted like sweet wrappers', in paragraph 6?

   A It shows that the iron looked like sweet wrappers.

   B It shows the destructive power of the cyclone.

   C It helps you to imagine what the iron would look like when twisted.

   D It helps you to imagine how all the iron is still scattered about.

17 What is the author suggesting when he calls the route to the volcano 'the Road to Hell'?

   A The journey to the volcano is a terrible experience.

   B The journey to the volcano is like walking through Hell.

   C Seeing the volcano is like looking into the fires of Hell.

   D Seeing the volcano makes you think you're going to die.

18 Which of these is neither stated nor implied in paragraph 6 as an effect of the cyclone?

   A Buildings damaged

   B Plants damaged

   C Sheets of corrugated iron twisted

   D Locals killed

CONTINUE WORKING

19 In paragraph 7, what is meant by the word 'mesmeric'?

    A People can't stop looking at the magma.

    B People can't bring themselves to look at the magma.

    C People will never forget the sight of the magma.

    D People find the sight of the magma terrifying.

20 What does the writer mean in paragraph 7 when he suggests that the volcano 'defies rational explanation'?

    A The power of the volcano is very impressive.

    B The power of the volcano needs a scientific explanation.

    C The power of the volcano seems supernatural or godlike.

    D The power of the volcano is aggressive and volatile.

21 The writer uses personification in the phrase, 'watching as Mother Earth gives fiery birth'.

What is personification?

    A When something non-human is described using human qualities.

    B When nature is compared to an object.

    C When nature is used to represent human emotions.

    D When a person is written about using references to nature.

22 In paragraph 8, what do John's friends do as soon as he has stopped talking?

    A Ask lots of questions

    B Hastily take photographs of the volcano

    C Start to go quickly back down the mountain

    D Move closer to the rim of the volcano for a better look

23 Which of these best describes the word 'awe' in the context of paragraph 8?

    A Fear and wonder

    B Surprise and excitement

    C Love and respect

    D Admiration and disbelief

CONTINUE WORKING

24 **What surprises the writer at the end of the passage?**

   A John has not been to any other volcanoes.

   B John's eyes gleam devilishly.

   C John was only guessing about how to get to the volcano.

   D John will never visit a volcano again.

25 **What does the writer mean at the end of the passage when he says John 'qualifies his answer'?**

   A John confirmed that he was a fully qualified geologist.

   B John explained his answer further.

   C John changed his first answer.

   D John gave an official answer.

STOP AND WAIT FOR FURTHER INSTRUCTIONS

SECTION 2: ODD ONE OUT

 INSTRUCTIONS

 YOU HAVE 6 MINUTES TO COMPLETE THE FOLLOWING SECTION.

YOU HAVE 24 QUESTIONS TO COMPLETE WITHIN THE TIME GIVEN.

Example i

Four of these words are related in some way. Select the word that does not go with the other four.

A	B	C	D	E
modest	huge	gigantic	enormous	massive

The correct answer is **A**. This has already been marked in Example i in Section 2 of your answer sheet on page 159.

Example ii

Four of these words are related in some way. Select the word that does not go with the other four.

A	B	C	D	E
rush	walk	hurry	dash	dart

The correct answer is **B**. Mark the answer B in Example ii in Section 2 of your answer sheet on page 159.

STOP AND WAIT FOR FURTHER INSTRUCTIONS

In each set, four of the words are related in some way. Select the word that does not go with the other four.

1

A	B	C	D	E
cornet	trombone	tuba	violin	trumpet

2

A	B	C	D	E
pebble	stone	boulder	rock	soil

3

A	B	C	D	E
cut	slice	rip	seal	tear

4

A	B	C	D	E
tiny	great	small	miniscule	minute

5

A	B	C	D	E
gold	diamond	silver	copper	iron

6

A	B	C	D	E
leaf	tree	branch	bark	twig

7

A	B	C	D	E
line	row	quarrel	argument	dispute

8

A	B	C	D	E
boot	sole	slipper	trainer	sandal

CONTINUE WORKING

9	A	B	C	D	E
	puppy	cub	kitten	goat	foal

10	A	B	C	D	E
	major	minor	corporal	general	colonel

11	A	B	C	D	E
	dictionary	atlas	thesaurus	manual	novel

12	A	B	C	D	E
	wood	copse	forest	plant	orchard

13	A	B	C	D	E
	walk	stroll	saunter	hop	wander

14	A	B	C	D	E
	level	flat	uniform	even	irregular

15	A	B	C	D	E
	beautiful	pretty	jolly	handsome	gorgeous

16	A	B	C	D	E
	tigress	mare	vixen	boar	ewe

CONTINUE WORKING

17

A	B	C	D	E
drag	lift	elevate	hoist	raise

18

A	B	C	D	E
make	produce	provisions	food	supplies

19

A	B	C	D	E
professor	teacher	solicitor	lecturer	tutor

20

A	B	C	D	E
carry	bring	transport	vehicle	fetch

21

A	B	C	D	E
spectacles	periscope	binoculars	optician	telescope

22

A	B	C	D	E
rucksack	wallet	holdall	briefcase	satchel

23

A	B	C	D	E
nurse	surgeon	reporter	doctor	porter

24

A	B	C	D	E
novice	specialist	master	virtuoso	maestro

STOP AND WAIT FOR FURTHER INSTRUCTIONS

SECTION 3: ANTONYMS

 YOU HAVE 6 MINUTES TO COMPLETE THE FOLLOWING SECTION.

YOU HAVE 24 QUESTIONS TO COMPLETE WITHIN THE TIME GIVEN.

Example i

Select the word that is least similar in meaning to the following word:

light

A	B	C	D	E
dark	water	feather	bright	hill

The correct answer is **A**. This has already been marked in Example i in Section 3 of your answer sheet on page 160.

Example ii

Select the word that is least similar in meaning to the following word:

smooth

A	B	C	D	E
allow	beneath	rough	whilst	shade

The correct answer is **C**. Mark the answer C in Example ii in Section 3 of your answer sheet on page 160.

STOP AND WAIT FOR FURTHER INSTRUCTIONS

In each question, select the word from the table that is least similar in meaning to the word above the table.

1 climb

A	B	C	D	E
descend	clamber	hike	scale	mount

2 final

A	B	C	D	E
last	stage	latest	original	centre

3 loyal

A	B	C	D	E
unfriendly	faithful	disloyal	illogical	improper

4 tame

A	B	C	D	E
wild	energetic	interesting	great	fast

5 careful

A	B	C	D	E
cautious	casual	determined	lazy	untidy

6 brief

A	B	C	D	E
durable	interval	slow	boring	long

7 plump

A	B	C	D	E
slimy	speedy	average	scrawny	tall

8 accumulate

A	B	C	D	E
consolidate	reach	disperse	hold	gather

CONTINUE WORKING

9 sweet

A	B	C	D	E
plain	chewy	spicy	tasty	sour

10 ambitious

A	B	C	D	E
illusive	immoral	standard	unambitious	mismanage

11 unkempt

A	B	C	D	E
tidy	short	dense	shallow	cleaned

12 offspring

A	B	C	D	E
generation	cousin	sibling	peer	parent

13 stationary

A	B	C	D	E
written	random	moving	sloping	halt

14 bliss

A	B	C	D	E
satisfaction	misery	danger	worry	delight

15 disgrace

A	B	C	D	E
honour	brave	loyalty	kind	courage

16 complex

A	B	C	D	E
tough	network	simple	centre	problematic

CONTINUE WORKING

17 guilt

A	B	C	D	E
despair	innocence	hope	regret	dignity

18 cooperate

A	B	C	D	E
regain	convince	behave	prevent	oppose

19 fertile

A	B	C	D	E
rugged	overgrown	barren	lush	sandy

20 harmony

A	B	C	D	E
tranquillity	conflict	belief	noise	horror

21 commemorate

A	B	C	D	E
remember	argue	surprise	ignore	salute

22 sever

A	B	C	D	E
simple	maintain	destroy	start	join

23 feeble

A	B	C	D	E
meek	strong	useful	vivid	gaudy

24 abundance

A	B	C	D	E
shortage	loss	sufficient	extinction	reliance

STOP AND WAIT FOR FURTHER INSTRUCTIONS

SECTION 4: WORD ASSOCIATION

 INSTRUCTIONS

 YOU HAVE 6 MINUTES TO COMPLETE THE FOLLOWING SECTION.

YOU HAVE 24 QUESTIONS TO COMPLETE WITHIN THE TIME GIVEN.

Example i

Select the word that is most closely associated to the following word:

telephone

A	B	C	D	E
necklace	watch	bracelet	charm	ring

The correct answer is **E**. This has already been marked in Example i in Section 4 of your answer sheet on page 160.

Example ii

Select the word that is most closely associated to the following word:

bunch

A	B	C	D	E
trees	keys	oranges	sweets	apples

The correct answer is **B**. Mark the answer B in Example ii in Section 4 of your answer sheet on page 160.

STOP AND WAIT FOR FURTHER INSTRUCTIONS

In each question, select the word from the table that is most closely associated to the word above the table.

1 leopard

A	B	C	D	E
spies	sees	looks	spots	stares

2 rank

A	B	C	D	E
ships	taxis	buses	cars	bicycles

3 treasure

A	B	C	D	E
shoulder	rib	trunk	chest	neck

4 hay

A	B	C	D	E
pile	heap	bale	pack	sack

5 important

A	B	C	D	E
sergeant	corporal	major	colonel	private

6 little

A	B	C	D	E
jelly	portion	ice-cream	trifle	dessert

7 knock

A	B	C	D	E
pipe	tap	leak	tank	sink

8 carpenter

A	B	C	D	E
plane	balloon	drone	helicopter	jet

CONTINUE WORKING

9 obstruct

A	B	C	D	E
pack	hamper	picnic	basket	spread

10 type

A	B	C	D	E
kind	generous	helpful	gracious	decent

11 bread

A	B	C	D	E
crumble	tumble	shake	roll	rock

12 can

A	B	C	D	E
plastic	iron	bronze	tin	lead

13 seal

A	B	C	D	E
cub	kitten	pup	calf	fry

14 castle

A	B	C	D	E
maintain	preserve	hold	keep	retain

15 heart

A	B	C	D	E
leather	silk	bronze	silver	gold

16 opinion

A	B	C	D	E
scene	view	panorama	outlook	prospect

CONTINUE WORKING

17 amphibian

A	B	C	D	E
trout	snake	frog	perch	mole

18 bend

A	B	C	D	E
sandal	heel	buckle	shoe	sole

19 setback

A	B	C	D	E
gale	blow	shove	gust	push

20 detective

A	B	C	D	E
box	folder	file	bag	case

21 shape

A	B	C	D	E
calculate	figure	reckon	image	shadow

22 lose

A	B	C	D	E
shed	hut	cabin	hutch	hide

23 odds

A	B	C	D	E
tops	sides	ends	bottoms	beginnings

24 eggs

A	B	C	D	E
snatch	grasp	seize	clutch	pinch

STOP AND WAIT FOR FURTHER INSTRUCTIONS

SECTION 5: CLOZE

 INSTRUCTIONS

 YOU HAVE 6 MINUTES TO COMPLETE THE FOLLOWING SECTION.

YOU HAVE 14 QUESTIONS TO COMPLETE WITHIN THE TIME GIVEN.

Example i

Complete the sentence in the most sensible way by selecting the appropriate word from each set of brackets.

The (dog, big, gate) sat on the (mat, open, great).

A   big, open
B   dog, great
C   gate, mat
D   dog, mat
E   dog, open

The correct answer is **D**. This has already been marked in Example i in Section 5 of your answer sheet on page 160.

Example ii

Complete the sentence in the most sensible way by selecting the appropriate word from each set of brackets.

My name is (Imran, high, sand) and I am (eleven, dig, land) years old.

A   Imran, dig
B   high, land
C   sand, land
D   Imran, land
E   Imran, eleven

The correct answer is **E**. Mark the answer E in Example ii in Section 5 of your answer sheet on page 160.

STOP AND WAIT FOR FURTHER INSTRUCTIONS

Complete each sentence in the most sensible way by selecting the appropriate combination of words from within the brackets. Use one word from each set of brackets.

1 The (nurse, librarian, builder) calmly explained that he needed to check my (savings, temperature, speed).

   A librarian, speed

   B nurse, savings

   C builder, speed

   D nurse, temperature

   E librarian, savings

2 (Although, Despite, Following) a torrential downpour, the school sports day was (cancelled, developed, unsuccessful).

   A Despite, developed

   B Following, developed

   C Following, cancelled

   D Despite, cancelled

   E Although, unsuccessful

3 The (cows, horses, geese) congregated nervously at the starting (barn, door, gate), waiting for the race to (commence, finish, appear).

   A cows, barn, finish

   B horses, gate, commence

   C geese, door, appear

   D horses, door, finish

   E cows, gate, finish

4 With no time to (finish, lose, begin) the experienced pilot landed the plane before the second (steward, engine, trolley) caught fire.

   A lose, engine

   B begin, steward

   C lose, steward

   D finish, trolley

   E begin, trolley

CONTINUE WORKING

5 After (mourning, morning, meaning) the loss of his pet (rabbit, aunt, car), Ben was relieved to get into (bath, bed, state).

   A morning, rabbit, bath

   B meaning, aunt, state

   C mourning, car, bath

   D mourning, rabbit, bed

   E meaning, aunt, bed

6 The (athlete, internet, construction) pulled a (nail, ladder, muscle) during the hurdles.

   A internet, nail

   B athlete, ladder

   C athlete, muscle

   D construction, ladder

   E internet, muscle

7 (Whomever, Whoever, Who) left this nasty note is (well, clearly, rapidly) unpleasant.

   A Whomever, well

   B Whoever, well

   C Whomever, rapidly

   D Whoever, clearly

   E Who, clearly

8 We held our (shoulders, yawns, breath) as we waited for the Head Teacher to (cry, announce, distribute) the winner.

   A shoulders, announce

   B yawns, distribute

   C breath, cry

   D shoulders, distribute

   E breath, announce

CONTINUE WORKING

9 A low (crane, aeroplane, bridge) links the island to the (boat, bonfire, mainland) but can be flooded at (low, high, wide) tide.

    A bridge, mainland, high

    B aeroplane, boat, high

    C bridge, mainland, low

    D crane, bonfire, high

    E crane, boat, wide

10 The (music, letters, audience) applauded the musicians who gave their (notes, instruments, all) to the performance.

    A letters, notes

    B audience, instruments

    C audience, all

    D music, instruments

    E letters, all

Questions 11–14

In this passage, some of the words are missing. Complete the passage by selecting the best set of words for each question. Mark your answer on the answer sheet by choosing one of the options A–E. Each set of words can only be used once.

The boy ran through the village as night fell. The hunters were close behind. | **Question 11** | and was surprised when the door opened by itself. The cottage appeared to be empty though | **Question 12** | which were two rustic chairs. Outside he could hear shouts and the sounds of pounding feet. He climbed the narrow staircase into a bedroom. He now heard loud hammering on the door below. | **Question 13** | he noticed a small hatchway between the oak beams. Standing on tiptoe, he was able to push the hatch open and pull himself upwards. As he replaced the hatch, he could hear steps on the narrow stairs. The first hunter raised the hatch and scanned the loft. | **Question 14** | above which was a small skylight in the roof: it was open.

A	It was empty but for an old trunk
B	The occupants of the cottage had obviously returned.
C	a fire was burning in the hearth on either side of
D	He came to an old cottage and rapped on the door
E	Looking up to the low ceiling,

END OF PAPER

Collins

11+
Verbal
Reasoning

Answers

For the CEM test

Answers

Revision Answers

Pages 8–9: Skimming and Scanning Text

1 C
As the text is about two girls playing netball seeing someone trying to steal a car, this would be the best title out of the answer options.

2 D
The expression 'quick-witted' means acting or reacting in a mentally quick way.

Pages 10–13: Finding Information

1 C
The narrator tells us explicitly that it is a 'seven-person crew'.

2 B
One crew member says they had to abandon their goal of 'making it to Hawaii'.

3 D
The narrator tells us explicitly that the journey is a copy of one made 'more than a thousand years ago'.

4 C
The baby is described as sitting on the rug, 'its nappy forming a solid base'.

5 C
The narrator tells us that Dom holds the toys out of the baby's reach, which implies he doesn't like the baby.

Pages 14–15: Organisation of Text

1 A
Subheadings and bullet points can help organise a non-fiction text so that it is clear and concise.

2 D
The subheading 'More Mystery' is a clue; also, the fact that scientists can't explain it.

Pages 16–17: Understanding Context

1 A
This is a commonly used opening to fairy tales.

2 C
'Knowing they were poor' tells us that this is the reason the girl asked for only a rose.

Pages 20–21: Information Retrieval Questions

1 D
The journey is described as 'long and tedious, with lengthy delays on the M6'.

2 D
The narrator's son is pulling at his arm and calling 'Dad'.

Pages 22–23: Understanding Meaning Questions

1 B
The first line explicitly summarises what the article is about.

2 D
The lines: 'When all at once I saw a crowd, A host, of golden daffodils' are a clue; from this point on, the poem continues to describe the daffodils.

3 A
There were so many daffodils they seemed to go on and on like the stars; also, their colour is bright yellow so the poet is comparing them to the shining, twinkling stars on the Milky Way.

Pages 24–27: Inference and Deduction Questions

1 B
The reader can infer from the text that it is because Gwendoline is able to wave goodbye to her mother.

2 C
The narrator implies that Gwendoline's mother has been crying by referring to her 'moist cheeks', so we can infer she was sad.

3 D
The narrator implies that she has been crying as we are told earlier that 'Gwendoline sobbed'.

Pages 28–29: Language Definition Questions

1 B
The word 'innocence' can mean a lack of guilt; it can also mean inexperienced and therefore unaware of the bad things in life, as in this passage.

2 B
As 'larger-than-life' means 'unusual', its opposite meaning here is 'ordinary'.

Pages 30–31: Author's Intentions and Use of Language Questions

1 D
The words 'skitter' and 'hot pursuit' both refer to fast movement.

2 A
The narrator explicitly refers to 'rustling' and 'loud chewing' coming from the kitchen.

Pages 32–33: Parts of Speech Questions

1 Proper noun: Sylvie; three nouns: gloves, tights, hat; three adjectives: green, blue, woolly

2 Pronoun: he; verb: played; adverb: quietly

3 Three prepositions: across, under, into; conjunction: and

Pages 34–35: Literary Technique Questions

1 The poisonous mushroom looked like a sinister umbrella

2 a) personification
   b) rhyme
   c) onomatopoeia
   d) simile

Pages 36–37: Spelling, Grammar and Punctuation

1 a) **m m o**   accommodate
   b) **r a s**   embarrassment
   c) **c i o**   conscious

2 preferred, spotting
The final 'r' of 'prefer' should be doubled when adding the suffix -ed as the 'fer' syllable is still stressed.
The final 't' of 'spot' should be doubled when adding the suffix -ing because 'spot' has a short vowel sound.

3 enjoys; gives; capture; experience

Pages 38–39: Word Definitions

1 D unrelated
2 A fiercely
3 C walking
4 E dispute

Pages 40–41: Odd One Out

1 D constant
The other words give a sense of what is 'usual' or 'commonplace', whereas 'constant' suggests something that is ever-present.

2 B mix
The other words indicate a sense of 'organising' something, whereas 'mix' suggests the opposite.

Pages 42–43: Synonyms and Antonyms

1 C waterfall
The word 'waterfall' is the best synonym among the choices given.

2 A narrow
The word 'narrow' is the best antonym among the choices given.

Pages 44–45: Word Association

1 E electric
The homophone 'currant' could link to some of the other options, but 'electric' is the only option associated with 'current'.

2 B coat
The other options are types of coat but only 'coat' is associated with 'paint' (i.e. a coat of paint).

Pages 46–47: Cloze

1   C cities
2   A banks
3   E parks
4   I culture
5   F fascinating
6   D divided
7   B built
8   J travelling
9   G families
10 H torn

Page 48: Shuffled Sentences

1 **D** through
The correct sentence is 'Max threw the necklace out of the kitchen window in a rage'.

2 **B** impression
The correct sentence is 'The sales job was tougher than Brogan had been led to believe'.

Practice Answers

Pages 50–53
Practice Test 1: Comprehension

1 **A**
Botswana

2 **C**
'Did you sleep well?'

3 **C**
Using sprays or nets.

4 **D**
To remind us to be remorseful for our mistakes (the passage says 'Bad consciences, it would appear, are there for a purpose: to make us feel regret over our failings.')

5 **A**
10 p.m.

6 **B**
Because they are tired from a hard day's work (the passage says 'Mechanics in general sleep well, as do many others whose day is taken up with physically demanding labour.').

7 **B**
Options 2 and 4 only (Mma Makutsi sitting at her desk and driving her vehicle).

8 **B**
How to tend to cows (the passage says 'explaining to her about the ways of cattle, a subject that he knew so well.').

9 **D**
Quench

10 **D**
They were close (the passage says 'so many memories and sayings and observations, that she, his daughter, could now call up and cherish').

Pages 54–57
Practice Test 2: Comprehension

1 **D**
The girl was sitting.

2 **D**
Robust (the passage says 'She was not a dainty thing but a good-size farm girl.').

3 **A**
Nervous (the passage says 'The storm makes you skittish.').

4 **B**
The Witch thought it would help her get the measure of the girl (the passage says 'Was she to be taken seriously, or was she merely a blow-away dandelion seed, caught on the wrong side of the wind? If she could see the girl's face, the Witch felt she might know.').

5 **A**
Clumsily (the passage says 'She was up and running in an ungainly way')

6 **C**
Simile

7 **C**
She could not venture out in the rain (the passage says 'The Witch could not venture out in such a vicious, insinuating wetness').

8 **B**
She had faced many obstacles and setbacks (the passage says 'The punishing political climate of Oz had beat her down, dried her up, tossed her away').

9 **B**
Imminent

10 **B**
Decreasing

Pages 58–61
Practice Test 3: Comprehension

1 **B**
politics, social issues and crime

2 **C**
Build a relationship with the source

3 **A**
They need to be eager to find out things.

4 **D**
In case the story they are covering is distressing.

5 **A**
Media organisations

6 **B**
They harass their subjects (the passage says 'Paparazzi are unpopular as they invade their subjects' privacy.').

7 **C**
unprepared

8 **D**
Simile

9 **B**
stalking

10 **D**
following

Pages 62–65
Practice Test 4: Comprehension

1 **B**
Options 1 and 4 (the second paragraph refers to the western neighbours Iceland and Greenland).

2 **D**
Baltic Sea ('The Swedish Vikings set out across the Baltic Sea into Northern Europe').

3 **C**
Viking head-dresses

4 **A**
Options 1 and 4 ('Plutarch, writing in the first century AD, describes Northern Europeans as dressing up with head-dresses that resemble wild beasts, and a ninth-century tapestry in Oseberg, Norway, shows a man wearing a set of horns.').

5 **B**
The priests who wrote them didn't like the fact that they were heathens (paragraph five supports this answer).

6 **B**
They didn't try to spread their religion.

7 **C**
products

8 **A**
They brought valuable commodities and helped build up farming communities (the last two sentences of the final paragraph support this answer).

9 **B**
adjectives

10 **C**
The Viking – friend or foe? (the final paragraph suggests that the Vikings might have had a more positive influence than historical accounts of their aggression would make us believe).

Pages 66–68
Practice Test 5: Grammar and Spelling

1 **B**
2 **D**
3 **D**
4 **C**
5 **B**
6 **E**
7 **D**
The correct spelling is 'rhythm'.
8 **B**
The correct spelling is 'desperate'.
9 **C**
The correct spelling is 'calendar'.
10 **B**
The correct spelling is 'grateful'.
11 **A**
The correct spelling is 'separate'.
12 **e d i**   immediately
13 **s t r**   disastrous
14 **e r r**   interrupt
15 **e r n**   government
16 **d r a**   hindrance

Pages 69–71
Practice Test 6: Synonyms

1 **C** permit
2 **E** empty
3 **B** clever
4 **D** untrue
5 **A** happy
6 **E** enormous
7 **C** faithful
8 **D** noisy
9 **E** courteous
10 **B** scarce
11 **D** genuine
12 **D** leave
13 **C** wealthy
14 **B** impolite
15 **E** secure

Pages 72–74
Practice Test 7: Antonyms

1 **D** before
2 **C** ugly
3 **B** loser
4 **D** compliment
5 **E** forbid
6 **D** abundance
7 **E** senior
8 **A** cruel
9 **B** broad
10 **C** never
11 **B** complicated
12 **D** careless

13   C   particular
14   E   war
15   C   natural

Pages 75–77
Practice Test 8: Definitions
1   C   buy
'To purchase' something is to buy it.
2   A   inside
The interior of a building is the inside part.
3   E   bravery
'Courage' and 'bravery' are synonyms.
4   D   pulled
'To haul' is to pull or drag something or someone.
5   A   unoccupied
'Vacant' means 'not occupied' or 'empty'.
6   B   luxurious
'Lavish' means 'grand' or 'ornate'.
7   E   twisted
The facial features become twisted or stretched if they 'contort'.
8   B   surrender
'To yield' is to give up or surrender.
9   A   immediately
'Promptly' means 'without delay', i.e. immediately.
10   C   agreed
'To approve' something is to give agreement to it.
11   B   continue
In this context, 'to proceed' means to carry on or continue the journey.
12   E   care
In this context, 'caution' means 'care'.
13   C   criticised
'To rebuke' someone is to tell them off or criticise them.
14   D   chances
The nouns 'opportunity' and 'chance' are often synonymous.
15   C   speechless
'Tongue-tied' means unable to speak.
16   B   scowled
'Glowered' means to stare angrily.

Pages 78–80
Practice Test 9: Word Association
1   D   ruler
A 'ruler' can also mean someone who rules or governs a country.
2   E   lions
Pride is the collective noun for lions.
3   E   charm
'Lucky charm' is a common phrase.
4   D   manners
Children may be expected to show good table manners at meals.
5   E   star
Celebrities are often 'stars' of film or TV.
6   C   volume
'Volume' is also another term for a book.
7   B   peeled
'Keeping one's eyes peeled' means to watch something or someone carefully.

8   D   crane
The sole function of a crane is to lift things.
9   A   sheep
Sheep are gathered into a pen.
10   B   churn
A churn is also a large metal container for milk.
11   A   fingers
Tactile relates to the sense of touch.
12   E   humour
A joke is an example of humour.
13   D   museum
A museum is the place to find out about the past.
14   A   speech
An oration is a formal kind of speech.
15   C   sharp
'Razor sharp' is a common way of saying 'extremely sharp'.
16   B   train
Both 'coach' and 'train' are used for teaching sport, etc.

Pages 81–83
Practice Test 10: Odd One Out
1   B   swimming
The other sports all take place on dry land.
2   E   sugar
The other foodstuffs are all dairy products.
3   B   bowl
The other containers are cuboid-shaped.
4   C   frown
The other words all express happiness or pleasure.
5   C   brain
The other parts of the body are all bony.
6   A   pea
The other vegetables all grow below ground.
7   E   usual
The other adjectives all describe something unusual.
8   A   pig
The other words all relate to crop cultivation.
9   B   honest
The other words can all describe good weather.
10   E   scene
The other words are all ways of seeing.
11   C   polyester
The other materials are all natural, not man-made.
12   B   detect
The other words all relate to 'following'.
13   C   gale
The other words all relate to rainfall.
14   E   cottage
The other words identify settlements rather than an individual home.
15   B   rapid
The other words are all bird types.

16   D   reach
The other words all imply movement in an upwards direction.

Pages 84–86
Practice Test 11: Shuffled Sentences
1   D   eaten
The boy ate the apple.
2   A   ate
Sarah was eight years old.
3   C   flight
The car sped along the road.
4   B   animals
The farmer grew his crops.
5   D   timing
We had lots of homework.
6   B   lifted
The desk was made of wood.
7   D   dislike
Most of the students enjoyed the course.
8   B   to
She made too many mistakes.
9   E   gaze
The wind blew through the forest.
10   D   open
Noah loved his friends and family. OR Noah loved his family and friends.
11   E   into
The young boy ran quickly.
12   B   capability
The city's inhabitants were upset.
13   D   figure
Frequent exercise can help prevent illness.
14   A   four
The lawyer summarised the case for the jury.
15   D   suffer
The prisoner attacked his fellow inmates.

Pages 87–89
Practice Test 12: Cloze
1   F   essential
2   C   strong
3   E   absorbed
4   I   directly
5   D   adequate
6   A   minutes
7   G   deficiency
8   J   brittle
9   B   found
10   H   pills
11   C   fought
12   I   army
13   A   estimate
14   G   forces
15   E   morning
16   F   flee
17   D   crowned
18   B   death
19   H   significant
20   J   attempts

Pages 93–118
ASSESSMENT PAPER 1
Section 1: Comprehension (pages 95–102)

1 **C**
In the window, there are lots of different bottles plus signs saying what Krook buys and sells. Only one picture is referred to, the books are on a table outside the shop, and the sacks are on the floor inside the shop.

2 **B**
The narrator adds, 'Everything seemed to be bought and nothing to be sold there'.

3 **D**
'There were several second-hand bags, blue and red, hanging up'.

4 **A**
'Dirty' suggests unclean (matching A, C, and D); 'hanger-on' and 'disowned' suggests not being wanted (rather than busyness or clothes).

5 **B**
Krook only sells empty wine bottles not the actual wine.

6 **D**
The narrator notes how many keys there are but focuses on their rust (there is no mention of them being in a chest), 'all the rusty keys, of which there must have been hundreds huddled together as old iron'.

7 **C**
'Discoloured' suggests their age while 'dog's-eared' means the corners have been folded over.

8 **A**
Richard jokes that the pile of bones belongs to people rather than animals.

9 **D**
'Intercept' means to stop or block; the wall stops light reaching the shop, leaving the last 'couple of yards' in front of the shop in darkness. Elsewhere, the text reinforces how dark it is inside the shop.

10 **B**
Leading to the simile, Krook is described as 'short, cadaverous, and withered […] His throat, chin, and eyebrows were so frosted with white hairs'.

11 **C**
He is wearing spectacles but carrying a lamp, 'a lighted lantern that an old man in spectacles and a hairy cap was carrying about in the shop'.

12 **A**
Eccentric means unusual or strange (the old woman refers to Krook as 'odd'); the colloquial form of 'funny' could suggest this but 'surprising' does not match.

13 **A**
The old woman is introducing them to Krook. 'Gave' and 'delivered' would suggest some sense of movement or exchange, while 'exhibit' implies a more formal display.

14 **B**
The phrase 'her lofty station' and 'great stateliness' suggest she is behaving in a self-important way. She suggests he is mad, not herself.

15 **B**
Krook laughs at and discusses the nickname, suggesting it is not cruel. Krook is much lower in social status than a Lord Chancellor, suggesting irony. Hyperbole would suggest he already has a lot of social status and it is being exaggerated. A simile would require the comparison to use 'like' or 'as'.

16 **D**
In the text, it is used to describe the verb 'said'.

17 **A**
Krook describes its 'colour' and 'texture'.

18 **D**
'She shook her head a great many times and tapped her forehead with her finger […] "For he is a little—you know—M!"'.

19 **B**
He claims to have 'three sacks of ladies' hair below'.

20 **C**
Although Richard's behaviour could be seen as loving, the way he stops Krook touching Ada's hair suggests protectiveness. His speech is formal and assertive rather than romantic.

21 **B**
Referring to Krook touching Ada's hair, Richard tells him to, '"admire as the rest of us do without taking that liberty."'

22 **D**
'Darted' could suggest the 'suddenly' of A or the 'quickly' of D but it is specifically linked to how Krook looks at Richard.

23 **A**
Although she laughs, the text implies this is out of politeness and embarrassment. Before this, the author refers to Krook's behaviour as causing Ada to be 'startled and blushing'.

24 **C**
In the preceding sentence, Krook appears as if he is about to become aggressive with Richard; this causes Ada to speak and pretend she hasn't been offended.

25 **A**
The adverb 'suddenly' and the contrasting verbs 'shrunk' and 'leapt' suggest his behaviour quickly changes. The verb 'leap' could suggest B but it is meant metaphorically rather than an actual movement.

Section 2: Synonyms (pages 103–106)

1 **E** instruction
2 **B** chaperone
3 **C** container
4 **D** deflect
5 **E** idea
6 **A** determined
7 **A** dense
8 **C** sceptical
9 **E** negativity
10 **D** surrender
11 **A** unoccupied
12 **E** controlled
13 **B** spread
14 **D** unlawful
15 **A** playful
16 **E** glisten
17 **D** harmless
18 **C** supporter
19 **C** imply
20 **A** exploit
21 **C** basic
22 **C** gathering
23 **B** faulty
24 **E** hindrance

Section 3: Definitions (pages 107–110)

1 **D** enough
'Sufficient' means to have enough or the right amount.

2 **B** essential
If something is 'necessary', you need to have it.

3 **D** order
'Prescribe' means to write an order for medication which the pharmacist will carry out.

4 **B** medicine
'Medication' refers to any type of medicine.

5 **E** lawyer
A solicitor is a legal practitioner.

6 **C** regret
'Remorse' and 'regret' are synonyms.

7 **D** miserable
Dismal and miserable are similarly used to describe very poor weather.

8 **C** delayed
'To postpone' means 'to delay'.

9 **A** praised
'To acclaim' means 'to praise enthusiastically'.

10 **C** accomplishment
A feat is an accomplishment or achievement.

11 **C** paraded
In this context, 'to process' means 'to move in a procession' so 'paraded' is the correct option.

12 **D** crowd
In this context, a 'multitude' means 'many people' so 'crowd' is the correct choice.

13 **E** separated
'To detach' means 'to separate'.

14 **B** shrink
The verb 'to contract' is the opposite of 'to expand' so 'shrink' is the answer.

15 **D** hike
A 'trek' is a long 'hike'.

16 **A** cover
The term 'canopy' is used for many kinds of overhead covering.

17 **D** powerful
'Potent' means powerful, strong.

18 **B** cure
A 'remedy' is a cure (e.g. for illness) or a solution (e.g. to a problem).

19 **D** element
A 'factor' is a contributing part or element of a whole or in a process.

20 B release
A 'discharge' is the release of something or someone.

21 B noted
'Renowned' means 'celebrated' or 'noted' for a talent or an achievement.

22 D hold
'Sustain' means to hold, maintain or keep up.

23 A unrivalled
'Unsurpassed' means 'not attained by any other' so 'unrivalled' is the appropriate option.

24 C recognition
An 'accolade' is recognition or a tribute given to someone for their work.

Section 4: Shuffled Sentences (pages 111–114)

1 C indication
Mum has been telling us about her childhood in Kerala.

2 A picture
They took the dog along the towpath for her morning walk.

3 A lights
The inner city traffic has been unbelievably heavy today.

4 C flower
Finally Freya added flour to the butter and egg mixture.

5 D apart
The children went outside although it was raining heavily.

6 E petals
Ali put the roses in a glass vase and filled it with water.

7 D effecting
The nature programme showed how global warming is affecting the Arctic.

8 A hot
It was so cold we had to put on our hats and coats.

9 C upset
He tried to get his teacher's attention many times but without success.

10 B garage
We were quite upset when our neighbours decided to move abroad ('we' and 'our neighbours' can be interchanged).

11 E plane
The captain moored the boat at the quayside.

12 B wait
The shelf collapsed under the weight of so many books.

13 C at
Jake has invited me to his party but I don't want to go.

14 A last
Maire couldn't wait to see her two cousins from Australia.

15 D easy
The runners were exhausted after the gruelling race.

16 C desperate
Val's new computer means she is able to work much faster.

17 D are
We need a professional cleaner for our blocked chimney.

18 B people
It's important to have a balanced diet and plenty of exercise.

19 E queen
We discussed the life of Henry VIII after watching the documentary.

20 A captain
With barely a minute to spare they boarded the plane ('they boarded the plane' can instead be used at the start of the sentence).

21 C pushing
The builders are taking a long time to complete the extension.

22 E holiday
The school fair raised an amazing amount of money for our new playground ('the' and 'our' can be interchanged).

Section 5: Cloze (pages 115–118)

1	H	conquer
2	E	labyrinth
3	F	prison
4	B	soldiers
5	A	sets
6	C	Crete
7	J	soared
8	D	view
9	I	stone
10	G	death
11	G	object
12	D	granted
13	F	heritage
14	E	travesty
15	A	wildlife
16	C	congestion
17	B	issue
18	I	accept
19	J	think
20	H	response
21	C	led to a huge, thick metal door
22	E	when the door clanged shut
23	B	were all the same down here.
24	A	on which were writing materials including a quill.
25	A	occupied by a cone-shaped, metallic object
26	E	after six months spent on the International Space Station
27	B	as the capsule re-entered the earth's atmosphere.
28	C	or it could have completely burned up.

Pages 119–144
ASSESSMENT PAPER 2
Section 1: Comprehension (pages 121–128)

1 B
The geologist is described as talking 'casually' while the frightened tourists 'hug their knees' and have 'their eyes screwed up tight'.

2 D
The phrase describes their dangerous position rather than something that is specifically going to happen to them.

3 A
Although he describes the lava as 'noxious' in the first paragraph, it is only B–D that are mentioned in the second paragraph.

4 B
While answer A mentions the noise ('roar'), it doesn't cover the word 'omnipresent' which suggests something that is always there.

5 A
He refers to John as his 'new geologist acquaintance'. The word 'acquaintance' suggests someone you know but are not especially close to.

6 B
The writer describes using the rim of the crater as both a 'handrail' and a 'shield'.

7 C
Although the words link to anger (answer A), the writer isn't actually suggesting the volcano has human emotions. He is using personification to suggest how dangerous this active volcano is.

8 D
John explains that 'the magma is illuminating that ash cloud, which makes it look much worse than it actually is'.

9 C
The image of putting his arm around them suggests comfort but the metaphor shows that this comforting isn't actually a physical act. There may be some confusion with answer B as that is also about 'making them all feel better' but the arm image does not suggest 'pretending'.

10 B
The writer points out that, with 'the right vehicle', people can get within 200 metres (but then they would have to walk).

11 D
'Smoke and mirrors' refers to an illusion; when the writer says 'it's not real', he is referring to the sense of danger rather than the physical existence of the volcano.

12 A
The writer describes, 'the remote island of Tanna in the South Pacific archipelago of Vanuatu'.

13 D
He is describing the landscape that leads to the volcano.

14 B
The geographical feature is named after a Hawaiian goddess (answer A) but the feature itself is created from 'airborne molten lava caught by the wind and spun out into delicate strands'.

15 B
The writer describes the eruptions as being 'nearly continuously'.

16 B
Although the simile does say that the iron looked like 'sweet wrappers' (answer A) and helps the reader to imagine its appearance (answers C and D), the intended effect is to show the power of the cyclone.

17 C
The nickname focuses on what the road leads to, rather than the appearance of the road itself.

18 D
The passage mentions locals rebuilding and replanting but not their deaths.
19 A
'Mesmeric' suggests something is hypnotic or that it transfixes the onlooker.
20 C
Throughout the text, the writer links the volcano to different gods. By saying it 'defies rational explanation', he is implying that the volcano contains some power that is beyond human understanding.
21 A
22 C
The writer says that John's friends, 'beat a hasty retreat back around the rim's circumference and down to the base'.
23 A
Although there could be some confusion with answers C and D (as 'awe' suggests respect arising from fear and wonder), the writer does not indicate that he either loves or admires the volcano.
24 A
John admits it is the 'first' volcano he has visited.
25 B
John explains why he has never visited a volcano before despite knowing so much about them.

Section 2: Odd One Out (pages 129–132)
1 D violin
The other words are names of brass instruments.
2 E soil
The others words are differently-sized stones.
3 D seal
The other words are all to do with dividing something.
4 B great
The other words all describe 'smallness'.
5 B diamond
The others are all metals.
6 B tree
The others are all tree parts.
7 A line
The other words all relate to disputes.
8 B sole
The other words are all types of footwear.
9 D goat
The other options are all names for the young of animals.
10 B minor
The other words are all ranks in the army.
11 E novel
The other options are all types of non-fiction, reference books.
12 D plant
The other words all refer to groupings of trees.
13 D hop
The other words all relate to two-legged styles of walking.
14 E irregular
The other words all describe regular, even surfaces.

15 C jolly
The other adjectives describe outward appearance, not personality.
16 D boar
The other words are names of female animals.
17 A drag
The other words all involve moving something upwards.
18 A make
The other words are all used to refer to foodstuffs.
19 C solicitor
The other words refer to professionals in education.
20 D vehicle
The other words refer to the action of conveying people or goods.
21 D optician
The other words are all types of visual equipment.
22 B wallet
The other words are all types of bags.
23 C reporter
The other words refer to people who work in hospitals.
24 A novice
The other words refer to people who have expertise in an area.

Section 3: Antonyms (pages 133–136)
1 A descend
2 D original
3 C disloyal
4 A wild
5 B casual
6 E long
7 D scrawny
8 C disperse
9 E sour
10 D unambitious
11 A tidy
12 E parent
13 C moving
14 B misery
15 A honour
16 C simple
17 B innocence
18 E oppose
19 C barren
20 B conflict
21 D ignore
22 E join
23 B strong
24 A shortage

Section 4: Word Association (pages 137–140)
1 D spots
A leopard is marked by spots on its coat.
2 B taxis
A line of waiting taxis or their base is called a rank.
3 D chest
Pirates were reputed to bury their treasure in chests.
4 C bale
Hay is gathered into 'bales' (by machines) when harvested.
5 C major
Major (adjective) means important; major (noun) is a military rank.

6 D trifle
A 'trifle' is a dessert but can also mean a small amount.
7 B tap
To give something a tap is to give it a small knock.
8 A plane
A plane is a tool used by carpenters to shave wood.
9 B hamper
'Hamper' (verb) is to obstruct; hamper (noun) is a large basket.
10 A kind
'Kind' (noun) is a synonym of 'type' or 'sort'.
11 D roll
Bread rolls are a bakery product.
12 D tin
The nouns 'tin' and 'can' can both refer to metal containers.
13 C pup
The young of seals are called pups.
14 D keep
The noun 'keep' refers to the main part of a castle.
15 E gold
Someone with a 'heart of gold' is by nature very good and kind to others.
16 B view
Your 'view' on an issue is your opinion on it.
17 C frog
Frogs are amphibians; the others are not.
18 C buckle
The verb 'to buckle' means to bend or collapse.
19 B blow
To suffer a 'blow' to one's hopes is to have a setback to them.
20 E case
A 'case' can also be the crime or matter a detective is investigating.
21 B figure
A 'figure' can be a shape or outline (as in a 'human figure').
22 A shed
The verb 'to shed' means to lose (for example weight, leaves).
23 C ends
'Odds and ends' is an expression meaning small objects of different kinds.
24 D clutch
The clutch for more than one egg laid in a nest is 'clutch'.

Section 5: Cloze (pages 141–144)
1 D nurse, temperature
2 C Following, cancelled
3 B horses, gate, commence
4 A lose, engine
5 D mourning, rabbit, bed
6 C athlete, muscle
7 D Whoever, clearly
8 E breath, announce
9 A bridge, mainland, high
10 C audience, all
11 D He came to an old cottage and rapped on the door
12 C a fire was burning in the hearth on either side of
13 E Looking up to the low ceiling,
14 A It was empty but for an old trunk

Progress Charts

Track your progress by shading in your score at each attempt.

Assessment Papers

	Score	Date:	Attempt 1	Paper 1: Section 1
/25	Score	Date:	Attempt 2	Comprehension
/24	Score	Date:	Attempt 1	Paper 1: Section 2
/24	Score	Date:	Attempt 2	Synonyms
/24	Score	Date:	Attempt 1	Paper 1: Section 3
/24	Score	Date:	Attempt 2	Definitions
/22	Score	Date:	Attempt 1	Paper 1: Section 4
/22	Score	Date:	Attempt 2	Shuffled Sentences
/28	Score	Date:	Attempt 1	Paper 1: Section 5
/28	Score	Date:	Attempt 2	Cloze
/25	Score	Date:	Attempt 1	Paper 2: Section 1
/25	Score	Date:	Attempt 2	Comprehension
/24	Score	Date:	Attempt 1	Paper 2: Section 2
/24	Score	Date:	Attempt 2	Odd One Out
/24	Score	Date:	Attempt 1	Paper 2: Section 3
/24	Score	Date:	Attempt 2	Antonyms
/24	Score	Date:	Attempt 1	Paper 2: Section 4
/24	Score	Date:	Attempt 2	Word Association
/14	Score	Date:	Attempt 1	Paper 2: Section 5
/14	Score	Date:	Attempt 2	Cloze

Practice Tests

	Score	Date:	Attempt 1	Practice Test 1:
/10	Score	Date:	Attempt 2	Comprehension
/10	Score	Date:	Attempt 1	Practice Test 2:
/10	Score	Date:	Attempt 2	Comprehension
/10	Score	Date:	Attempt 1	Practice Test 3:
/10	Score	Date:	Attempt 2	Comprehension
/10	Score	Date:	Attempt 1	Practice Test 4:
/10	Score	Date:	Attempt 2	Comprehension
/16	Score	Date:	Attempt 1	Practice Test 5:
/16	Score	Date:	Attempt 2	Grammar and Spelling
/15	Score	Date:	Attempt 1	Practice Test 6:
/15	Score	Date:	Attempt 2	Synonyms
/15	Score	Date:	Attempt 1	Practice Test 7:
/15	Score	Date:	Attempt 2	Antonyms
/16	Score	Date:	Attempt 1	Practice Test 8:
/16	Score	Date:	Attempt 2	Definitions
/16	Score	Date:	Attempt 1	Practice Test 9:
/16	Score	Date:	Attempt 2	Word Association
/16	Score	Date:	Attempt 1	Practice Test 10:
/16	Score	Date:	Attempt 2	Odd One Out
/15	Score	Date:	Attempt 1	Practice Test 11:
/15	Score	Date:	Attempt 2	Shuffled Sentences
/20	Score	Date:	Attempt 1	Practice Test 12:
/20	Score	Date:	Attempt 2	Cloze

Pupil's Full Name:

Instructions:
Mark the boxes correctly like this ✎

Please sign your name here:

Practice Test 1: Comprehension

Example i

| | A | ~~B~~ | C | D |

Example ii

| | A | B | C | D |

1	A	B	C	D
2	A	B	C	D
3	A	B	C	D
4	A	B	C	D
5	A	B	C	D
6	A	B	C	D
7	A	B	C	D
8	A	B	C	D
9	A	B	C	D
10	A	B	C	D

Practice Test 3: Comprehension

Example i

| | ✶ | B | C | D |

Example ii

| | A | B | C | D |

1	A	B	C	D
2	A	B	C	D
3	A	B	C	D
4	A	B	C	D
5	A	B	C	D
6	A	B	C	D
7	A	B	C	D
8	A	B	C	D
9	A	B	C	D
10	A	B	C	D

Practice Test 2: Comprehension

Example i

| | A | ~~B~~ | C | D |

Example ii

| | A | B | C | D |

1	A	B	C	D
2	A	B	C	D
3	A	B	C	D
4	A	B	C	D
5	A	B	C	D
6	A	B	C	D
7	A	B	C	D
8	A	B	C	D
9	A	B	C	D
10	A	B	C	D

Practice Test 4: Comprehension

Example i

| | ✶ | B | C | D |

Example ii

| | A | B | C | D |

1	A	B	C	D
2	A	B	C	D
3	A	B	C	D
4	A	B	C	D
5	A	B	C	D
6	A	B	C	D
7	A	B	C	D
8	A	B	C	D
9	A	B	C	D
10	A	B	C	D

Practice Test 5: Grammar and Spelling

Example i

	A	B	C	D	E

Example ii

	A	B	C	D	E
1	A	B	C	D	E
2	A	B	C	D	E
3	A	B	C	D	E
4	A	B	C	D	E
5	A	B	C	D	E
6	A	B	C	D	E
7	A	B	C	D	E
8	A	B	C	D	E
9	A	B	C	D	E
10	A	B	C	D	E
11	A	B	C	D	E
12	—	—	—		
13	—	—	—		
14	—	—	—		
15	—	—	—		
16	—	—	—		

Practice Test 6: Synonyms

Example i

	A	B	C	D	E

Example ii

	A	B	C	D	E
1	A	B	C	D	E
2	A	B	C	D	E
3	A	B	C	D	E
4	A	B	C	D	E
5	A	B	C	D	E
6	A	B	C	D	E
7	A	B	C	D	E
8	A	B	C	D	E
9	A	B	C	D	E
10	A	B	C	D	E
11	A	B	C	D	E
12	A	B	C	D	E
13	A	B	C	D	E
14	A	B	C	D	E
15	A	B	C	D	E

Practice Test 7: Antonyms

Example i

	A	B	C	D	E

Example ii

	A	B	C	D	E
1	A	B	C	D	E
2	A	B	C	D	E
3	A	B	C	D	E
4	A	B	C	D	E
5	A	B	C	D	E
6	A	B	C	D	E
7	A	B	C	D	E
8	A	B	C	D	E
9	A	B	C	D	E
10	A	B	C	D	E
11	A	B	C	D	E
12	A	B	C	D	E
13	A	B	C	D	E
14	A	B	C	D	E
15	A	B	C	D	E

Practice Test 8: Definitions

Example i

	A	B	C	D	E
	A	B	C	D	E

Example ii

	A	B	C	D	E
	A	B	C	D	E
1	A	B	C	D	E
2	A	B	C	D	E
3	A	B	C	D	E
4	A	B	C	D	E
5	A	B	C	D	E
6	A	B	C	D	E
7	A	B	C	D	E
8	A	B	C	D	E
9	A	B	C	D	E
10	A	B	C	D	E
11	A	B	C	D	E
12	A	B	C	D	E
13	A	B	C	D	E
14	A	B	C	D	E
15	A	B	C	D	E
16	A	B	C	D	E

Practice Test 9: Word Association

Example i

	A	B	C	D	E

Example ii

	A	B	C	D	E
1	A	B	C	D	E
2	A	B	C	D	E
3	A	B	C	D	E
4	A	B	C	D	E
5	A	B	C	D	E
6	A	B	C	D	E
7	A	B	C	D	E
8	A	B	C	D	E
9	A	B	C	D	E
10	A	B	C	D	E
11	A	B	C	D	E
12	A	B	C	D	E
13	A	B	C	D	E
14	A	B	C	D	E
15	A	B	C	D	E
16	A	B	C	D	E

Practice Test 10: Odd One Out

Example i

	A	B	C	D	E

Example ii

	A	B	C	D	E
1	A	B	C	D	E
2	A	B	C	D	E
3	A	B	C	D	E
4	A	B	C	D	E
5	A	B	C	D	E
6	A	B	C	D	E
7	A	B	C	D	E
8	A	B	C	D	E
9	A	B	C	D	E
10	A	B	C	D	E
11	A	B	C	D	E
12	A	B	C	D	E
13	A	B	C	D	E
14	A	B	C	D	E
15	A	B	C	D	E
16	A	B	C	D	E

Practice Test 11: Shuffled Sentences

Example i

	A	B	C	D	E

Example ii

	A	B	C	D	E
1	A	B	C	D	E
2	A	B	C	D	E
3	A	B	C	D	E
4	A	B	C	D	E
5	A	B	C	D	E
6	A	B	C	D	E
7	A	B	C	D	E
8	A	B	C	D	E
9	A	B	C	D	E
10	A	B	C	D	E
11	A	B	C	D	E
12	A	B	C	D	E
13	A	B	C	D	E
14	A	B	C	D	E
15	A	B	C	D	E

Practice Test 12: Cloze

Example i

	A	B	C	D	E

Example ii

	A	B	C	D	E
1	A	B	C	D	E	F	G	H	I	J
2	A	B	C	D	E	F	G	H	I	J
3	A	B	C	D	E	F	G	H	I	J
4	A	B	C	D	E	F	G	H	I	J
5	A	B	C	D	E	F	G	H	I	J
6	A	B	C	D	E	F	G	H	I	J
7	A	B	C	D	E	F	G	H	I	J
8	A	B	C	D	E	F	G	H	I	J
9	A	B	C	D	E	F	G	H	I	J
10	A	B	C	D	E	F	G	H	I	J
11	A	B	C	D	E	F	G	H	I	J
12	A	B	C	D	E	F	G	H	I	J
13	A	B	C	D	E	F	G	H	I	J
14	A	B	C	D	E	F	G	H	I	J
15	A	B	C	D	E	F	G	H	I	J
16	A	B	C	D	E	F	G	H	I	J
17	A	B	C	D	E	F	G	H	I	J
18	A	B	C	D	E	F	G	H	I	J
19	A	B	C	D	E	F	G	H	I	J
20	A	B	C	D	E	F	G	H	I	J

THIS PAGE HAS DELIBERATELY BEEN LEFT BLANK

Pupil's Full Name:

Instructions:
Mark the boxes correctly like this ✖

Please sign your name here:

Section 1: Comprehension

Example i

	A	B	C	D

Example ii

	A	B	C	D
1	A	B	C	D
2	A	B	C	D
3	A	B	C	D
4	A	B	C	D
5	A	B	C	D
6	A	B	C	D
7	A	B	C	D
8	A	B	C	D
9	A	B	C	D
10	A	B	C	D
11	A	B	C	D
12	A	B	C	D
13	A	B	C	D
14	A	B	C	D
15	A	B	C	D
16	A	B	C	D
17	A	B	C	D
18	A	B	C	D
19	A	B	C	D
20	A	B	C	D
21	A	B	C	D
22	A	B	C	D
23	A	B	C	D
24	A	B	C	D
25	A	B	C	D

Section 2: Synonyms

Example i

	A	B	C	D	E

Example ii

	A	B	C	D	E
1	A	B	C	D	E
2	A	B	C	D	E
3	A	B	C	D	E
4	A	B	C	D	E
5	A	B	C	D	E
6	A	B	C	D	E
7	A	B	C	D	E
8	A	B	C	D	E
9	A	B	C	D	E
10	A	B	C	D	E
11	A	B	C	D	E
12	A	B	C	D	E
13	A	B	C	D	E
14	A	B	C	D	E
15	A	B	C	D	E
16	A	B	C	D	E
17	A	B	C	D	E
18	A	B	C	D	E
19	A	B	C	D	E
20	A	B	C	D	E
21	A	B	C	D	E
22	A	B	C	D	E
23	A	B	C	D	E
24	A	B	C	D	E

Section 3: Definitions

Example i

	A	B	C	D	E

Example ii

	A	B	C	D	E

#	A	B	C	D	E
1	A	B	C	D	E
2	A	B	C	D	E
3	A	B	C	D	E
4	A	B	C	D	E
5	A	B	C	D	E
6	A	B	C	D	E
7	A	B	C	D	E
8	A	B	C	D	E
9	A	B	C	D	E
10	A	B	C	D	E
11	A	B	C	D	E
12	A	B	C	D	E
13	A	B	C	D	E
14	A	B	C	D	E
15	A	B	C	D	E
16	A	B	C	D	E
17	A	B	C	D	E
18	A	B	C	D	E
19	A	B	C	D	E
20	A	B	C	D	E
21	A	B	C	D	E
22	A	B	C	D	E
23	A	B	C	D	E
24	A	B	C	D	E

Section 4: Shuffled Sentences

Example i

	A	B	C	D	E

Example ii

	A	B	C	D	E

#	A	B	C	D	E
1	A	B	C	D	E
2	A	B	C	D	E
3	A	B	C	D	E
4	A	B	C	D	E
5	A	B	C	D	E
6	A	B	C	D	E
7	A	B	C	D	E
8	A	B	C	D	E
9	A	B	C	D	E
10	A	B	C	D	E
11	A	B	C	D	E
12	A	B	C	D	E
13	A	B	C	D	E
14	A	B	C	D	E
15	A	B	C	D	E
16	A	B	C	D	E
17	A	B	C	D	E
18	A	B	C	D	E
19	A	B	C	D	E
20	A	B	C	D	E
21	A	B	C	D	E
22	A	B	C	D	E

Section 5: Cloze

Example i

	A	B	C	D	E

#	A	B	C	D	E	F	G	H	I	J
1	A	B	C	D	E	F	G	H	I	J
2	A	B	C	D	E	F	G	H	I	J
3	A	B	C	D	E	F	G	H	I	J
4	A	B	C	D	E	F	G	H	I	J
5	A	B	C	D	E	F	G	H	I	J
6	A	B	C	D	E	F	G	H	I	J
7	A	B	C	D	E	F	G	H	I	J
8	A	B	C	D	E	F	G	H	I	J
9	A	B	C	D	E	F	G	H	I	J
10	A	B	C	D	E	F	G	H	I	J
11	A	B	C	D	E	F	G	H	I	J
12	A	B	C	D	E	F	G	H	I	J
13	A	B	C	D	E	F	G	H	I	J
14	A	B	C	D	E	F	G	H	I	J

Example ii

	A	B	C	D	E

#	A	B	C	D	E	F	G	H	I	J
15	A	B	C	D	E	F	G	H	I	J
16	A	B	C	D	E	F	G	H	I	J
17	A	B	C	D	E	F	G	H	I	J
18	A	B	C	D	E	F	G	H	I	J
19	A	B	C	D	E	F	G	H	I	J
20	A	B	C	D	E	F	G	H	I	J
21	A	B	C	D	E
22	A	B	C	D	E
23	A	B	C	D	E
24	A	B	C	D	E
25	A	B	C	D	E
26	A	B	C	D	E
27	A	B	C	D	E
28	A	B	C	D	E

Pupil's Full Name:

2

Instructions:
Mark the boxes correctly like this ▲

Please sign your name here:

Section 1: Comprehension

Example i

	A	B	C	D

Example ii

	A	B	C	D
1	A	B	C	D
2	A	B	C	D
3	A	B	C	D
4	A	B	C	D
5	A	B	C	D
6	A	B	C	D
7	A	B	C	D
8	A	B	C	D
9	A	B	C	D
10	A	B	C	D
11	A	B	C	D
12	A	B	C	D
13	A	B	C	D
14	A	B	C	D
15	A	B	C	D
16	A	B	C	D
17	A	B	C	D
18	A	B	C	D
19	A	B	C	D
20	A	B	C	D
21	A	B	C	D
22	A	B	C	D
23	A	B	C	D
24	A	B	C	D
25	A	B	C	D

Section 2: Odd One Out

Example i

	A	B	C	D	E

Example ii

	A	B	C	D	E
1	A	B	C	D	E
2	A	B	C	D	E
3	A	B	C	D	E
4	A	B	C	D	E
5	A	B	C	D	E
6	A	B	C	D	E
7	A	B	C	D	E
8	A	B	C	D	E
9	A	B	C	D	E
10	A	B	C	D	E
11	A	B	C	D	E
12	A	B	C	D	E
13	A	B	C	D	E
14	A	B	C	D	E
15	A	B	C	D	E
16	A	B	C	D	E
17	A	B	C	D	E
18	A	B	C	D	E
19	A	B	C	D	E
20	A	B	C	D	E
21	A	B	C	D	E
22	A	B	C	D	E
23	A	B	C	D	E
24	A	B	C	D	E

Section 3: Antonyms

Example i

	A	B	C	D	E

Example ii

	A	B	C	D	E
1	A	B	C	D	E
2	A	B	C	D	E
3	A	B	C	D	E
4	A	B	C	D	E
5	A	B	C	D	E
6	A	B	C	D	E
7	A	B	C	D	E
8	A	B	C	D	E
9	A	B	C	D	E
10	A	B	C	D	E
11	A	B	C	D	E
12	A	B	C	D	E
13	A	B	C	D	E
14	A	B	C	D	E
15	A	B	C	D	E
16	A	B	C	D	E
17	A	B	C	D	E
18	A	B	C	D	E
19	A	B	C	D	E
20	A	B	C	D	E
21	A	B	C	D	E
22	A	B	C	D	E
23	A	B	C	D	E
24	A	B	C	D	E

Section 4: Word Association

Example i

	A	B	C	D	E

Example ii

	A	B	C	D	E
1	A	B	C	D	E
2	A	B	C	D	E
3	A	B	C	D	E
4	A	B	C	D	E
5	A	B	C	D	E
6	A	B	C	D	E
7	A	B	C	D	E
8	A	B	C	D	E
9	A	B	C	D	E
10	A	B	C	D	E
11	A	B	C	D	E
12	A	B	C	D	E
13	A	B	C	D	E
14	A	B	C	D	E
15	A	B	C	D	E
16	A	B	C	D	E
17	A	B	C	D	E
18	A	B	C	D	E
19	A	B	C	D	E
20	A	B	C	D	E
21	A	B	C	D	E
22	A	B	C	D	E
23	A	B	C	D	E
24	A	B	C	D	E

Section 5: Cloze

Example i

	A	B	C	D	E
1	A	B	C	D	E
2	A	B	C	D	E
3	A	B	C	D	E
4	A	B	C	D	E
5	A	B	C	D	E
6	A	B	C	D	E
7	A	B	C	D	E

Example ii

	A	B	C	D	E
8	A	B	C	D	E
9	A	B	C	D	E
10	A	B	C	D	E
11	A	B	C	D	E
12	A	B	C	D	E
13	A	B	C	D	E
14	A	B	C	D	E